F

D0876190

AUG 2 1 2019

From Cradle to Classroom

From Cradle to Classroom

A Guide to Special Education for Young Children

Nicholas D. Young, Elizabeth Jean, and
Anne E. Mead

ROWMAN & LITTLEFIELD
Lanham • Boulder • New York • London

Published by Rowman & Littlefield
A wholly owned subsidiary of The Rowman & Littlefield Publishing Group, Inc.
4501 Forbes Boulevard, Suite 200, Lanham, Maryland 20706
www.rowman.com

Unit A, Whitacre Mews, 26-34 Stannary Street, London SE11 4AB

British Library Cataloguing in Publication Information Available

Library of Congress Cataloging-in-Publication Data

ISBN 978-1-4758-4252-4 (cloth)
ISBN 978-1-4758-4254-8 (electronic)

♾™ The paper used in this publication meets the minimum requirements of American National Standard for Information Sciences—Permanence of Paper for Printed Library Materials, ANSI/NISO Z39.48-1992.

Printed in the United States of America

Dedications

Nicholas D. Young

I wish to dedicate my contributions to this book to my son, Maxwell (Max). Of course, at fifteen years old and over six feet, two inches, he may not completely appreciate being singled out at the moment as my "baby." Max was born nearly 24 inches long and has contributed mightily to my grocery bill ever since. When he was a little over three years old, he told me, in response to a perceived injustice, that he would not be treated a certain way because he was a "horman bean." This has become somewhat of a joking point ever since. His early requests to jump on the "cramp" and "cream" when referencing the trampoline in our backyard are equally memorable. May Max find the life path that makes him happy and know that his family will be there to support, love, and encourage him along the way. And may craftsmen understand the need to make a few extra-large cradles for those of maximum size like him, who will come along from time to time.

Elizabeth Jean

To my grandchildren, Nathan and Kaley. They are bright shining stars in a big, crazy world. It is with great anticipation that I look forward to watching them grow from the infants they are now, to the preschoolers they will soon be, and the students they will become in the not-so-distant future. Their hopes and dreams are limited only by what they cannot imagine. My wish for them is to be brave, be bold, and be great.

Anne E. Mead

To all the teachers who work with children with special needs: may you have the courage to experience the joy children bring to your classroom and have the fortitude to continue to do your very best to plan for classrooms that are inclusive.

Contents

Foreword

The journey from cradle to classroom begins with so much hope and potential. From the moment of conception to the day a young child walks into the classroom for the first time and begins formal schooling, the foundation for future learning is laid. Every teacher, every learning opportunity to come, will involve an interaction between the child's social, cognitive, and physical self and will initially be limited or supported by the foundation of development that is built through experiences and interactions in the earliest years.

Like a set of nesting dolls, a child's development begins by bonding with its mother, expands to include the connections and experiences made within the extended family and the family environment, depends upon the ongoing awareness of the child's pediatrician and his or her collaboration with caregivers, and if needed, should include access to the network of early interventionists available to support early development.

This ecological model of child development recognizes that the child's family, school, community, and social and cultural context influence growth and development and must be considered and addressed when we are seeking to understand and support children and families as part of the assessment and intervention cycle (Losardo and Notari Syverson, 2011). Likewise, emerging brain science emphasizes the interconnectedness of the brain and the body and the influence of experience and culture on learning and development (National Scientific Council on the Developing Child [NSCDC], 2010a).

Our genetic beginnings may gift us with attributes or may leave us vulnerable to developmental difficulties. What is clear is that our early experiences, whether we are nurtured or not, impact the foundations of brain development in ways that may later influence how efficiently we process language, how resilient we are under stress, and how our attention and memory systems develop. Early development is a time of enormous potential and a time when stress and lack of appropriate stimulation and engagement can negatively impact our later ability to learn.

The network of relationships and experiences, within which the child's development is seen, understood, and responded to, form the early foundation for learning. Any breakdown in normal development, as well as in the network that supports the child, will bring that youngster to the door of kindergarten with less potential for success.

LANGUAGE DEVELOPMENT BEGINS IN INFANCY

Research suggests that foundational skills for later language development form in the first months of life as part of early brain development (Benasich, Choudhury, Realpe-Bonilla, and Roesler, 2014; Maassen, van der Leij, Maurits, and Zwarts, 2012). Animal studies suggest that there is a critical period in the early development of the auditory cortex and, at this critical time, experiences with language and genetic risk factors interact to determine how efficiently the temporal patterning of speech sounds is organized (Benasich and Choudhury, 2012). In the first months of life, infants construct a phonemic map of language sounds; processing, discriminating, and acquiring language begin at this early stage of development (Benasich and Choudhury, 2012).

A family history of learning disabilities puts a child at greater risk for developing them (Benasich and Fitch, 2012; Grigorenko, 2012; LoTurco, Tarkar, and Yue Che, 2012). Studies of children's processing speed, memory, and discrimination, from infancy (starting at six months of age) through age ten, indicate that infants of parents with a history of language-learning disorders had less efficient and rapid auditory processing abilities than same-age peers from control groups, and that this was highly predictive of later delayed language development (Benasich and Choudhury, 2012).

The tendency for dyslexia to run in families has been noted since the late 1800s (LoTurco et al., 2012). Research conducted in the 1950s that compared monozygotic and fraternal twins, and many subsequent studies, have established an increased risk for the inheritance of learning disabilities of between 30 percent and 75 percent, depending on the study (LoTurco et al., 2012; Marino, Mascheretti, Facoetti, and Molteni, 2012). Advances in the field of genetics have led to the identification of several genetic markers currently being researched through animal models. Researchers suggest that each child's specific genetics and the environment they grow up in together influence development and level of risk for learning disabilities (Hoff and Tian, 2005; Marino et al., 2012).

Students still struggling with reading by third grade are often identified with dyslexia. Ferrer et al. (2015) suggest that 17 percent to 21 percent of the school population experiences developmental dyslexia and that 80 percent of children identified with learning disabilities are identified with dyslexia. Having analyzed a sample of 414 children from the Connecticut Longitudinal study, Ferrer et al. (2015) concludes that the achievement gap between typical and dyslexic readers is present at first grade and persists, with very little change, into adolescence.

According to their analysis of assessment results for passage comprehension, word attack, and word identification skills, children with early signs of dyslexia, indicated by lower scores on achievement tests that assess early reading skills, continue to make progress at a rate similar to that of peers but are not able to catch up to those who begin first grade without delayed skills (Ferrer et al., 2015). The authors highlight the importance of engaging children in effective reading instruction as early as possible, as foundational skills are formed in preschool and kindergarten (Ferrer et al., 2015).

THE IMPACTS OF POVERTY AND TOXIC STRESS

The National Center for Education Statistics for the 2013 school year notes that 51 percent of students in public schools were from low-income families (Suitts, Barba, and Dunn, 2015); however, rates of child poverty are not consistent across states and race. For example, child-poverty rates range from 11 percent in New Hampshire to 31 percent in Mississippi; and 36 percent of African American children, 34 percent of American Indian children, and 31 percent of Hispanic children experienced poverty, while only 12 percent of non-Hispanic white children experienced this threat to their development (Administration for Children & Families [ACF], 2017a).

Almost 50 percent of poor children begin kindergarten with an early learning delay and face the challenge of achieving accelerated growth in order to catch up to same-age peers (Isaacs, 2012). The stakes are high for achieving optimal development; poverty poses significant challenges for children and families, and children of nonwhite races are disproportionately exposed to these early stressors (Fielding, Kerr, and Rosier, 2007).

Young children's brains establish foundational networks, or early brain architecture, in response to their environment and their relational experiences in those environments. The level and persistence of stress in a child's environment impacts brain development (NSCDC, 2010a; NSCDC, 2014). When young children are chronically exposed to toxic levels of stress, initial brain architecture anticipates ongoing stress by establishing heightened responses as a baseline stress response (NSCDC, 2010a; NSCDC, 2014).

When the body's stress response system habitually overreacts to stress, the risk of stress-related physical and mental illness is increased substantially (NSCDC, 2014). Much of what is known about the body's response to stress is based on animal research. This research suggests that cortisol plays a role in turning specific genes on and off and that "high levels of cortisol lead to changes in the hippocampus; an area of the brain involved in learning, memory, and stress response regulation" (NSCDC, 2014, p. 3).

With MRI scanning, researchers have observed structural changes in the brains of children who have experienced chronic stress, such as a smaller hippocampus, which has been associated with low self-esteem; a smaller prefrontal cortex, which has been associated with impulsiveness and poor executive function skills; and increased growth in the amygdala, which has been associated with increased anxiety and aggression (Davidson and McEwen, 2012).

While the brain changes based on experience throughout life, there are thought to be sensitive periods in development; as neural circuits are initially maturing, the chemical environment and the electrical processing of experience lead to adjustments in the genetics and architecture of the brain (NSCDC, 2007; NSCDC, 2010a). The National Scientific Center for the Developing Child (2010a) report explains that once circuitry patterns are formed, different and new experiences have difficulty taking shape; thus, it is important to take advantage of early experiences to ensure that brain circuits develop properly. Early nutrition, exposure to drugs and toxic chemicals, and interactions with the environment and caregivers all impact children's early brain development for better or worse (NSCDC, 2010a).

The body's stress response system is linked to the body's ability to regulate behavior, attention, and emotion, abilities also known as executive function skills (Babcock, 2014). Research suggests that children's executive function skills are impacted in unique ways, based on personal profiles of risk exposure (Li-Grining, 2007). Living in poverty heightens the chances that a child will experience toxic levels of stress due to persistent life experiences such as threatening neighborhoods, low-quality child care options, gang violence, lack of trust in neighbors, living in homes with electrical and plumbing problems, lack of access to quality health care, low levels of education, and high levels of unemployment (NSCDC, 2010b; NSCDC, 2012).

In addition to environmental stressors, psychosocial stressors such as depression, substance abuse, criminal behavior, and domestic violence contribute to early exposure to toxic stress (Li-Grining, 2007). Children who live in poverty and are regularly exposed to violence in their communities are at greater risk for experiencing behavior problems and post-traumatic stress disorder; physical challenges often related to anxiety, such as headaches and stomachaches; and psychological challenges, such as lower self-esteem and a reduced capacity to feel and express empathy (NSCDC, 2010b).

Executive function skills such as the ability to control impulses, to plan, and to maintain focused attention are developed through experience and over time.

Children are not born with these skills; they develop them, based on support and experience in their environments (NSCDC, 2011). These skills form the foundation upon which cognitive and social development occur and have been described as the "biological foundation for school readiness" (NSCDC, 2011, p. 4). Children with reduced executive function skills have difficulty following directions, show reduced academic achievement, and are at greater risk for behavioral challenges with teachers and peers (NSCDC, 2011).

While growing up in poverty has the potential to negatively impact early development, recent longitudinal research suggests that children growing up in such conditions, and who don't experience a delay in reading skills at grade three, graduate from high school at the same rate as their more affluent peers (Hernandez, 2012; NSCDC, 2010a). In this study, almost four thousand children and families were followed and assessed for ten years. Study results indicated that 89 percent of children growing up in poverty and reading proficiently by third grade graduated on time; while 88 percent of students growing up in poverty and not reading proficiently by third grade did not graduate (Hernandez, 2012). These findings underscore the importance of high-quality early education programs.

THE POTENTIAL OF THE EARLY YEARS

While young children are vulnerable to negative impacts from their environment, this same sensitivity allows them to learn new skills through high-quality intervention. For example, in the Chicago School Readiness Project, Head Start teachers were provided with year-long behavior management training and stress-reduction workshops, while the children in the program with significant behavioral challenges were provided one-on-one counseling support. The executive function skills of attention, inhibition, and impulsivity in children improved; vocabulary, letter naming, and math skills also showed improvement. This model combined ongoing professional training and support for teachers with specialized therapeutic support for children (Diamond and Lee, 2011).

If early intervention and child-find programs are working effectively, the most at-risk learners should be receiving early intervention services as needed from birth to age three and should be enrolled in public school preschool programs for up to three years before entering kindergarten. This represents a significant opportunity to support early development; yet, since 2009, 52 percent to 53 percent of children ages three to four were not in school programs (ACF, 2017a).

As a thirty-year early childhood practitioner with experience in early intervention, as well as in public and private preschool settings, I have seen the worst and the best of my chosen field.

As a public preschool teacher, I've sat in many meetings with families, describing the physical and chemical nature of learning, the implications of a child's consistent inability to focus his or her attention for learning, and the strategies we might employ to build on the child's skills while recognizing his or her challenges. At times, these same parents recognize their own learning challenges, often unaddressed over the span of their personal school experience, and their resolve to support their child strengthens within a system of collaboration and support.

Children's early development lays the foundation for all later learning. A broad system of support is needed to prevent negative impacts on early development and to capitalize on each child's potential. This will take an investment of support across public and private domains for children and families, an investment that research has shown brings a bounty of dividends (Bartik, 2014).

This book, which highlights the many facets of the early intervention system from birth to age five, offers practitioners, parents, administrators, graduate students, and policy makers alike an overview of the societal and programmatic imperatives and challenges we face in building a cohesive and functional system of child and family support. The topics covered in *From Cradle to Classroom: A Guide to Special Education for Young Children* give the reader a comprehensive overview of the issues and challenges that must be addressed to realize the most value for continued public investment in early childhood. Policy and law impact the resources available to children, families, and practitioners. Even when resources are available, linking children and families to quality assessment and intervention services can be a challenge.

The current research base that describes the significant ways that early experience impacts later potential is at once inspiring in its clarity and at the same time intimidating in its implications. Linking with families, providing interventions with an awareness of cultural context, and fostering development across the domains of physical, social, and cognitive development within a service delivery model that is as diverse as the families it serves are all addressed by the authors. This important resource will provide the complex overview needed to capitalize on this time of enormous potential.

Sue O'Reilly-McRae, EdD
Preschool Teacher and Special Educator
Conway Grammar School
Union 38 School District
Conway, Massachusetts

Preface

From Cradle to Classroom: A Guide to Special Education for Young Children is a book written for regular and special education teachers, school administrators, school psychologists, related educational personnel, day care providers, parents, graduate students, and policy makers who work on behalf of infants, toddlers, and preschoolers to ensure they are ready for formal education when they reach age five. It reflects a keen understanding that early interventions are most effective in reducing the potential for special education or other support services later on.

While a well-established educational pathway exists for school-age children, little has been written to help further understanding of the birth-to-five learning continuum. Our motivation for writing this book comes from the following:

- A desire to inform the reader that there is a defined and accessible protocol, mandated by federal law, to ensure infants, toddlers, and preschoolers have access to services and education.
- The belief that our youngest children with developmental delays or who are at risk deserve the best chance at developmental and academic success from the very beginning of life, and early intervention services provide the vehicle for this to happen.
- The knowledge that although infants and toddlers eligible for early intervention services ranged from 2 percent to 78 percent across the United States, only 1.5 percent to 9.96 percent were enrolled in approved programs. Four states—Massachusetts, New Hampshire, New Mexico, and West Virginia—include infants and at-risk toddlers in their eligibility criteria (Rosenberg, Robinson, Shaw, and Ellison, 2013).

- The understanding that 59 percent of preschoolers, or six out of ten, do not attend preschool. This point is more clearly made when one considers that young children who are at risk for future academic failure and those from low-income families will start kindergarten more than a full year behind their peers (U.S. Department of Education, 2015).
- Our interest in ensuring that families, practitioners, and educators work together, regardless of cultural, economic, or other differences, to find interventions and solutions to improve outcomes for our youngest children who have disabilities or who are at risk.

Research suggests that children who attend high-quality preschools and are from low-income families, have disabilities, are dual-language learners, or are homeless or in foster care are twice as likely to go to a postsecondary institution, 30 percent more likely to receive their diploma from high school, and 40 percent less likely to require special education services during their primary, middle, and secondary school experiences (Executive Office of the President of the United States, 2015; Reynolds, Temple, Robertson, and Mann, 2001; U.S. Department of Education, 2015; Yoshikawa et al., 2013).

These same children will commit fewer crimes, score better on readiness tests, have better social skills, and display fewer behavioral problems (Yoshikawa et al., 2013). Predictably, children who attend preschools show a long-term cost-benefit of more than eight dollars for every dollar spent, and over their lifetime will earn 1.3 percent to 3.5 percent more annually (Executive Office of the President of the United States, 2015).

It is important to understand the many facets that encompass infancy, toddlerhood, and preschool, beginning with the history and laws that protect and serve our youngest population, regardless of whether they have disabilities, are in foster care or are homeless, are dual-language learners, come from low-income families, or are typically developing peers.

The first part of the title of this volume, *From Cradle to Classroom*, was chosen intentionally to show that a continuum does exist, beginning at birth and continuing on into the classroom, while the second part, *A Guide to Special Education for Young Children*, describes how educators, related practitioners, and parents can assist in helping infants, toddlers, and preschoolers grow, develop, and learn, to ensure the best possible outcomes in elementary school and beyond.

Research shows the benefits of investing in early intervention and high-quality preschool as a way to mitigate educational gaps in learning and to improve the development of children across all domains (Executive Office of the President of the United States, 2015; Lynch and Vaghul, 2015; Yoshikawa et al., 2013). Throughout the book, readers will find strategies to help atypical children navigate the world as they move from infancy to toddlerhood, and to preschool and beyond. The chapters dig deep and offer expansive understandings of the components necessary to ensure young children, especially those with exceptionalities, become successful students.

Chapter 1 begins with a look at the history of early childhood education, beginning prior to the signing of the Elementary and Secondary Education Act and ending with a look at the agencies that watch over preschools and childcare facilities. Attention is given to research that recognizes the importance of high-quality preschools and to Head Start, the first federally funded early intervention for children of low-income families.

Child Find, the federal law responsible for identifying struggling children, evaluating them, and providing services if found eligible, is discussed in chapter 2. Other components include a look at the emotional rollercoaster that occurs in the family when a child is found eligible, an explanation of the Individualized Family Service Plan for children birth to age three, and the Individualized Education Plan for children over three, as well as the importance of service providers.

Chapter 3 takes an in-depth look at many of the factors that influence development after birth. One percent of all children age five and under in the United States have a disability (Kraus, 2017). These are often found when children do not meet normal developmental milestones, and, as a result, it is vital that the adults who are responsible ensure the best set of circumstances for growth (Centers for Disease Control [CDC], 2015).

Partnering with families is one of the most important steps educators and practitioners can do to help a struggling child. Chapter 4 looks at the connection between parent and practitioner, and considers the collaboration needed to ensure success for infants, toddlers, and preschoolers who need support during the formative years. This is accomplished by looking at a variety of engagement models, including the Home Visit Program.

Understanding that schools are becoming increasingly more diverse, chapter 5 looks at how to best serve dual-language learners in a culturally responsive way. Cultural barriers may exist at the outset of any relationship; however, the best educators and practitioners find ways to break through those walls and make connections that encourage collaboration and lead to academic and developmental gains for children.

Chapter 6 examines the physical and cognitive development of infants, toddlers, and preschoolers as they move from one stage to the next. Theories of development are explained, normal milestones are mentioned, and intervention strategies for supporting atypical development are described. Fostering growth in both domains leads to young children who are able to take on the rigors of an academic setting as they move from being preschoolers to primary school–age students.

Social-emotional development has purposefully been separated to allow for a deep discussion of how best to support atypical children; thus, chapter 7 examines the milestones most infants, toddlers, and preschoolers meet, as well as how to support parents as they develop bonds with their child. Supporting social-emotional growth through intensive interventions is also discussed.

Chapter 8 discusses the use of play as an educational intervention. Play is important because it is the primary context in which children learn socialization, social awareness, and acceptance. Typical children learn to play naturally; however, atypical children need support during play as they struggle to make friends, understand cues, and develop social skills.

Fostering speech and language development is the subject of chapter 9. Speech and language are actually two very different but intertwined processes; whereas speech is the use of sounds to make words, language is the use of words to put thoughts together. Infants, toddlers, and preschoolers who are exposed to vocabulary-rich homes and environments and thus larger vocabularies, and, not surprisingly, children who attend dual-language schools fare better academically, whether they are typical or atypical learners.

Looking ahead, chapter 10 examines the shift that comes after preschool and as children move into an even more rigorous academic setting. Transitions are difficult, and the traditional school environment may seem foreign to families who are used to a more inclusive preschool classroom; thus, it is important for educators to take the extra time to get to know these families. Wraparound services are also identified and explained.

In totality, this book offers a comprehensive look at all that is necessary to ensure success of children with exceptionalities, birth to age five, while understanding that typical peers will also benefit from the interventions and strategies suggested, and that they will boost the outcomes of the atypical population by merely being themselves.

As authors of this book, we have been connected to infants, toddlers, and preschoolers in a variety of ways. At different times in our collective history, one or more of us has been an early childhood administrator, daycare provider, special education administrator, early childhood educator, elementary principal, superintendent of schools, graduate professor, and researcher, and we are parents who understand the importance of preventing or minimizing academic and developmental challenges; thus, we appreciate the emotional investment that other early childhood and special educator enthusiasts have in this topic.

It is our hope that you, the reader, will come back to this book again and again as a resource and reference guide to lead you through the intricacies of the birth-to-five developmental continuum. We wish you the very best in your work with infants, toddlers, preschoolers, and parents. Last but not least, thank you for being an advocate for our youngest children—as the pages before you will soon explain, your efforts are both needed and worthwhile.

Acknowledgments

As always, we dedicate this book to Sue Clark, who has become an invaluable partner in our academic pursuits. Her attention to detail and careful questioning has undoubtedly improved this book beyond measure. We are grateful for her wisdom, time, and support.

Chapter 1

From Humble Beginnings

Understanding the History, Laws, and Importance of Early Childhood Education

From its auspicious beginnings in the 1960s to the influence of laws and decades of research, preschool as a means to combat poverty and increase developmental and academic outcomes has become a necessity. This was not always the case; however, many laws have since been put in place to safeguard children and services, beginning with the Elementary and Secondary Education Act of 1965 and Individuals with Disabilities Education Act, Part C (n.d.), as well as the most recent Every Student Succeeds Act of 2015 (Klein, 2016). The Early Reading First grant is also an important step toward ensuring literacy for all youngsters.

Children who come from disadvantaged backgrounds, have disabilities, or are at risk benefit from all that preschool offers. The High/Scope Perry Preschool Study (National Research Council, 2001), as well as several other important studies, laid the groundwork for the necessity of high-quality preschools. Head Start (Peak, 2015), the National Association for the Education of Young Children (n.d.), and the Quality Rating and Improvement System (National Center on Early Childhood Quality Assurance [NCECQA], n.d.) offer further discussion points on the importance of high-quality, meaningful early care and education practices for our youngest children.

THE HISTORY OF PRESCHOOL: LAWS AND PROGRAMS

As early as the 1900s, John Dewey and Maria Montessori began offering schools for young children, while at the same time, settlement houses offered social services to tenement residents as a way to circumvent poverty (Follari, 2015). When the U.S. Children's Bureau was created in 1912, it fought for a policy that supported stay-at-home mothers, as well as a pension for low-income mothers, as a way to ensure best care for infants (Michel, 2011). Unfortunately, poverty rates increased, so it became financially impractical for the government to provide such benefits.

As the Great Depression of the 1930s hit, "emergency nursery schools" were established to employ out-of-work teachers while offering free, government-sponsored schools to all children regardless of race, color, or class (Michel, 2011). Although only open for part of the day, these schools became childcare facilities as mothers attempted to make some money on work-relief projects. Toward the end of the 1930s, many teachers left the preschool field for better-paid work, and many of these child centers soon closed down (Follari, 2015; Michel, 2011). World War II forced a need for state-funded childcare as more women went to work, and Congress expanded childcare–based initiatives (Follari, 2015).

The 1960s was a time of great upheaval, and education was no exception. In 1965, Lyndon B. Johnson signed the Elementary and Secondary Education Act (ESEA) into action as part of his war on poverty; similarly, the Early Childhood Education Act (ECEA) was signed into law (U.S. Department of Education, 2014). Both laws were meant to reduce poverty, give equal access to education for all students, and, by doing so, create a generation of adults for whom financial stability was possible (Decker, 2016). The ECEA also outlined federal funding for preschools and kindergartens and described a set of services specific to children birth to age five (U.S. Department of Education, 2014).

The ESEA, however, fell far short of its goal to ensure high-quality education to all, especially to those who were poor or disabled, which meant that many would be subjected to a life of dependency and poverty (Decker, 2016). This new social movement influenced the beliefs of practitioners and scholars who fought for educational equality. At the same time that the ESEA was signed, Head Start was established by Jule Sugarman and Dr. Edward Zigler (Peak, 2015). An early intervention program, Head Start aimed to mitigate the effects of poverty in young children, hoping that educational outcomes would improve (Peak, 2015). Additionally, a series of laws and movements would impact services to young children.

In 1971, universal childcare was proposed to Congress in the form of the Comprehensive Child Development Act but was vetoed by President Nixon (Michel, 2011). Low-income families suffered for three decades and received only marginal help until the Child Care and Development Block Grant was passed in 1990 (Michel, 2011). The grant was reworked in 1996 and called the Child Care and Development Fund; however, this new grant used a combination of factors to determine benefits, and as a result, was more available to middle-income families than the low-income families for which it was originally intended (Michel, 2011).

The Education for All Handicapped Children Act (EHA) of 1975 is an important law to consider, as it ensures that children with disabilities are ensured fair and appropriate special education services that meet their needs (Young, Bonanno-Sotiropoulos, and Smolinski, 2018). The act requires public schools to provide equal access to education in the least restrictive environment. Families who feel schools have not upheld this mandate are able to dispute their claims, using protocols set by the school, to include due process (Young et al., 2018).

The National Association for the Education of Young Children (NAEYC) was created in 1985 as a voluntary accreditation program (National Association for the Education of Young Children [NAEYC], n.d.). Here the organization works to "connect early childhood practice, policy, and research" (NAEYC, n.d., n.p.) through professional development, accreditation, and sharing of resources. Similarly, the National Center on Early Childhood Quality Assurance (NCECQA, n.d.) created the Quality Rating and Improvement System (QRIS) in the early 1990s as a way to improve childcare and preschools.

The Individuals with Disabilities Education Act (IDEA) was a renamed version of the EHA that was signed into law in 1990 (Young et al., 2018). Several smaller iterations followed in both 1997 and 2004; however, the main content remained the same (Special Education News, 2017). There were four components to IDEA, with Parts C and B being the most pertinent to the discussion of early childhood:

Part A: Its purpose and relevant definitions
Part B: Requirements for public school for children age 3 to 21
Part C: Requirements for families with infants and toddlers, birth to age 2
Part D: Resources and national initiatives to improve special education
   (Special Education News, 2017)

Part B requires schools to educate all students equally, regardless of disability and in the least restrictive environment, but with typical peers when feasible (American Psychiatric Association, 2016; National Center for Learning Disabilities, 2014). Part C ensures that infants, toddlers, and their families are ready for preschool by providing services and measuring outcomes (U.S. Department of Education, n.d.a).

In 2001, ESEA was reauthorized and became known as "No Child Left Behind" (NCLB, 2002) and, for better or worse, made massive changes to education, including establishing high academic outcomes as the expectation for all students, even those with disabilities. Of note, students with disabilities increased in reading and math performance over a thirteen-year period through 2014 (Decker, 2016). As part of NCLB (2002), several programs were established, to include:

- The Early Reading First program: grants to fund model programs to prepare preschoolers and young children for school.
- Special Education Preschool Grants: funding to ensure three- to five-year-olds receive special education services.
- Special Education Grants for Infants and Families: assists with implementation of special education programs for children birth to age two who have disabilities.
- Early Childhood Educator Professional Development Program: a competitive grant that offers caregivers and educators a chance to develop skills specific to low-income areas.

The Preschool for All Initiative of 2013, built upon the idea that high-quality preschool should be promoted and expanded, offered more opportunities to three- and four-year-olds in low-income situations (First Five Years Fund, 2016). Together with the Preschool Development grant and home-visit program, the expectations for a multipronged focus on young learners who need access to high-quality education in order to improve outcomes was established (First Five Years Fund, 2016).

The Every Student Succeeds Act of 2015 is the third incarnation of ESEA. It rolls back much of the original intent of NCLB, but it does directly name the Preschool Development Grant program (Klein, 2016). The new take on this old program is that it focuses on broader access to high-quality early childhood education (Klein, 2016).

Based on research completed over several decades, the twenty-first century has brought a plethora of private and public preschools and childcare centers, many of which use public dollars to lower the cost and increase low-income student enrollment. Unfortunately, even with all the offerings, nationally only 29 percent of four-year-olds and 4 percent of three-year-olds attend free, high-quality public preschools.

RESEARCH STUDIES

A variety of research studies tout the importance of early learning programs as children, from low-income areas, with disabilities, or at risk who attend preschool tend to score better on readiness tests, have better social skills and fewer behavior problems, and, as teens and adults, are likely to commit fewer crimes (Aos et al., 2004; Barnett and Hustedt, 2003; Camilli, Vargas, Ryan, and Barnett, 2010; Gilliam and Zigler, 2001; Gormley, Phillips, and Gayer, 2008; Schweinhart et al., 2005; van Voorhis, Maier, Epstein, and Lloyd, 2013; Weiland and Yoshikawa, 2013; Yoshikawa et al., 2013). It is important; therefore, to understand the different research studies and what makes each important to the conversation surrounding early intervention.

New York and South Carolina Preschool Studies

The New York and South Carolina studies, both begun in the 1960s, offer a glimpse into two methodologically strong research projects on preschool programming. Positive effects from early intervention were proven to continue well into elementary school (Aos et al., 2004; Barnett and Masse, 2007; Gilliam and Zigler, 2001). Moreover, due to such services, there was a significant reduction of grade retention and special education referrals, while cognitive abilities rose and stabilized throughout elementary school (Aos et al., 2004; Barnett and Masse, 2007; Gilliam and Zigler, 2001).

Child Parent Center Study

The Child Parent Center (CPC) study was conducted in Chicago during the late 1960s and was the most comprehensive long-term research of large-scale public preschool. This model consisted of a half-day program for preschool and kindergarten, with an elementary component geared toward economically disadvantaged students (Besharov, Germanis, Higney, and Call, 2011; Bienia, 2016). More than half the students attended the program for two years, both as a three-year-old and a four-year-old, while the others attended only as a four-year-old (Reynolds et al., 2001).

The educator was licensed, and each room had an assistant as well as eighteen children: thus, the classroom ratio of one to nine (Reynolds et al., 2001). The CPC study ensured that the cost of the program, educational focus, staffing, and qualifications matched those of other high-quality state programs (Reynolds et al., 2001). Students in the CPC study received above-average outcome measures as compared to similarly aged peers not in this study (Reynolds et al., 2001).

Georgia and North Carolina Studies

Both states started universal preschools in 1993, and initial reports show that students were better prepared to begin kindergarten (Barnett and Hustedt, 2003). More recent studies show an increase in linguistic, cognitive, and social skills, and lasting gains though grade five (Duncan, 2015; Stancill, 2016). The Abecedarian project has continued with more positive results; for example, even at age twenty-one, the group exposed to high-quality early learning scored better on academic testing, and at age thirty, they were more likely to hold a job and have earned a bachelor's degree (Campbell, 2014).

Head Start and HighScope Studies

Two well-designed, longitudinal research studies whose outcomes are also noteworthy are the Tulsa and HighScope studies (Besharov et al., 2011; Schweinhart et al., 2005). The significance lies in the methodology used, the highly educated teachers hired, the ongoing professional development offered, and the mentorship given to all staff (Schweinhart et al., 2005). It is clear from the findings that programs that implement high standards and operate at exceptional levels produce high-quality preschools.

Head Start Pre-K Study

Universal preschool impacts all children almost identically, regardless of income, as this 1998 study of a Tulsa, Oklahoma, Head Start program proved (Lamy, Barnett, and Jung, 2006; Palmer, 2016). The Tulsa study highlighted the importance of teacher qualification and instructional focus as two main ingredients in improved student outcomes (Gormley et al., 2008).

Interestingly, the literacy and math scores for those children who attended Head Start were higher both at the beginning of kindergarten and when reviewed again in eighth grade, indicating the use of educational literacy standards and professional development made a difference (Bienia, 2016; Sanchez, 2016). An additional component is the requirement of families to participate in programming, which offers students a pathway to success (Sanchez, 2016).

High/Scope Perry Preschool Study

An experimental study, High/Scope Perry randomly placed 128 children who were considered both minority status and socioeconomically disadvantaged into one of two groups. The first went to half-day preschool and participated in home visits for two years, while the second had no preschool (Schweinhart et al., 2005). Class size was unusually small, with a ratio of 1:6, and the school spent more per student than most typically funded state programs (Schweinhart et al., 2005).

After two years in the program, the positive outcomes negated any previous issues, and the positive effects on achievement were substantial and continued through school (Bienia, 2016). The reading gap was closed by 40 percent by the students' nineteenth birthday, and at age forty, Perry Preschool participants boasted lasting improvements in employment and were less likely to be arrested (Heckman et al., 2010; Schweinhart et al., 2005).

HEAD START

Head Start, a government-funded and -run program, "promotes school readiness of children under 5 from low-income families through education, health, social, education, and other services" (U.S. Department of Health and Human Services, 2017, n.p.). What began in 1965 as a way to help economically disadvantaged children grew over time to include children with disabilities in 1972, dual-language learners in 1977, and the children affected by homelessness and foster care in 1992 (Administration for Children and Families [ACF], 2017a; Merrill, 2015). Whereas the original 1965 program included 561,000 children, in 2015 Head Start serviced 944,000 children, an increase of 62 percent (ACF, 2017a; Merrill, 2015).

In 1975, Head Start published the first set of performance standards that detailed guidelines for children ages three to five (Merrill, 2015). Several iterations later, the new performance standards are meant to strengthen their services to children with disabilities, those who are dual-language learners, children who are in foster care, and children and families who are homeless, while ensuring that children are ready for the rigor of elementary school and beyond (ACF, 2017c; Merrill, 2015).

Using a five-pronged approach, the standards include improving the impact of learning and development of infants, toddlers, and preschoolers, moving from a half-day/part-year program to a full-day/full-year program, building teacher skills to improve child outcomes, lesser focus on rules with greater focus on outcomes, and producing a greater taxpayer return on investment (ACF, 2017b). Specifically, the five performance standards include:

- **Promoting effective teaching and learning in all Head Start classrooms.** Teachers must teach a rigorous curriculum that is developmentally appropriate, including cognitive development, social and emotional well-being, and other learning as needed for school. Using the new learning outcomes framework, all teaching, curricula, and assessment is aligned, a teacher-mentor is provided, and there are clear limits on suspensions and removals as well as defined methods to return children to the classroom.
- **Expanding time for learning and healthy development.** Research has shown that disadvantaged children benefit from full-day and full-year programs more than half-day and part-year; thus, new standards for the amount of time children spend at a Head Start center have been updated to reflect this shift.
- **Maintaining and strengthening Head Start's comprehensive services and family engagement.** Family partnerships are an important part of Head Start and, as such, staff are required to pursue professional

development, maintain partnership agreements with families, make home visits, improve physical- and mental-health supports to families, provide dual-language systems, and help families with their role as the primary decision-making partner.

- **Ensuring the health and safety of Head Start children.** The new standards require programs to implement health and safety policies, practices, and procedures that include provisions for continuous improvement, ongoing training, and oversight and correction in order to keep children safe.
- **Promoting effective management and continuous improvement of Head Start programs.** Using data to improve programs, this standard helps to establish goals and measurable objectives to meet family and child needs, while ensuring privacy. It also expects that outcomes will take precedence over processes and plans, giving Head Start more say in how grants are used.

In totality, the standards are meant to provide a pathway to ensure high-quality, individualized services that support the healthy development of infants, toddlers, and preschoolers from low-income areas as well as those with disabilities, those in foster care or homeless, and those who are dual-language learners. Children involved with Head Start are able to reach their full potential, entering kindergarten at a level equal to their mid- and high-income peers (ACF, 2017a).

The NCECQA oversees the Quality Rating and Improvement System, which is another tool used by states and communities that want to improve their care centers and preschools. It is interesting to note that this organization is funded by the U.S. Department of Health and Human Services, and more specifically the Administration for Children and Families (which also runs Head Start).

QUALITY RATING AND IMPROVEMENT SYSTEM

Begun in the 1990s, the Quality Rating and Improvement System is a way to provide continuity between individual states to reward high-quality, accredited providers with more funds than nonaccredited providers (NCECQA, n.d.). QRIS is "a systemic approach to assess, improve, and communicate the level of quality" (NCECQA, n.d., n.p.) for early care facilities, preschools, and other education programs.

In essence, QRIS increases the quality of care and education, increases professional development for practitioners and providers, increases parent understanding and desire for quality care and education for their own children, creates a framework to link multiple facilities (such as Head Start,

Early Intervention programs, child care centers, etc.), and aligns systems and provides oversight (NCECQA, n.d.). Interestingly, providers that meet the lowest level requirements still have achieved a higher level of quality than those of similar organizations without accreditation (NCECQA, n.d.).

QRIS comprises five elements, each of which has several rating levels. They include:

1. Program standards that are used to provide the public, and parents specifically, with program-specific information and quality ratings.
2. Supports for program and practitioner, such as technical assistance, mentors, and training.
3. Financial incentives to improve learning environments, which improve ratings.
4. Quality assurance and monitoring meant to determine the degree to which programs are meeting QRIS standards.
5. A consumer-education framework that provides information and rating levels (NCECQA, n.d.).

The QRIS online resource guide provides eight links that can be used as tools for states that wish to move to a quality-rating system for early care and education facilities. QRIS activities can be paid for through funding from the federal Child Care and Development Fund (NCECQA, n.d.).

Another program that works specifically for infants, toddlers, and preschoolers is the National Association for the Education of Young Children (NAEYC). This organization defines itself as "promoting excellence in early childhood education" and uses a multipronged approach to improve developmental and educational outcomes for infants, toddlers, and preschoolers (NAEYC, n.d., n.p.).

NATIONAL ASSOCIATION FOR THE EDUCATION OF YOUNG CHILDREN

The National Association for the Education of Young Children is a professional community responsible for promoting high-quality learning for young children through age eight (NAEYC, n.d.). Accomplished through a deep connection between early childhood and practice, policy, and research, NAEYC discusses the importance of developmentally appropriate practices, early childhood program standards, and standards for professional preparation (Brown and Mowry, 2015; Lynch and Vaghul, 2015; NAEYC, n.d).

Similarly to Head Start, NAEYC touches on major topics in early childhood education such as curriculum, assessment and program evaluation, diversity, and issues related to dual-language learners and children with disabilities, using a series of position statements (NAEYC, n.d.). Preschools may choose to become NAEYC certified, a process that includes deep examination of the program and its staff, as well as its following strict regulations and expectations in a variety of standards (NAEYC, n.d.). NAEYC is also an accrediting body for high-quality preschools, a process that is detailed and requires much from its participants.

Curriculum, Assessment, and Program Evaluation

Curriculum, assessment, and program evaluation are important pieces of high-quality care and learning. In order to ensure that NAEYC clearly communicates its vision, the position paper discusses each piece individually. Curriculum must be thoughtfully planned, developmentally appropriate, culturally and linguistically responsive, challenging and engaging, and "likely to promote positive outcomes for all young children" (NAEYC, 2009b, p. 1).

A central part of any early childhood program must be a way to assess the program and outcomes, such as child progress, needs, and strengths (NAEYC, 2009b). As a way to accomplish this goal, NAEYC insists that assessments must be reliable, ethical, and developmentally appropriate (NAEYC, 2009b). Program evaluation and accountability must be regularly evaluated through the use of varied and sound evidence. Programs must meet predetermined, high-quality standards and should also examine any unintended outcomes in order to improve practice (NAEYC, 2009b, p. 2).

Developmentally Appropriate Practices

"Developmentally appropriate practices" refers to both meeting children where they are, as well as enabling them to work toward achievable yet challenging goals (Brown and Mowry, 2015; Lynch and Vaghul, 2015; NAEYC, 2009a). This means that learning experiences should be appropriate to children's ability level, age, and developmental stage, while taking into account their cultural and social contexts. It is not the practice of making things easy for children but instead providing opportunities that challenge children to promote their thinking and abilities (NAEYC, 2009a).

NAEYC developed a list of twelve principles of child development meant to inform teacher practice. The list is not all inclusive but demonstrates the interrelatedness of many learning and development aspects. Thus, it is necessary for the practitioner to look at the list broadly and infuse other influences as needed. The principles include:

- The domains of development and learning (social, emotional, cognitive, and physical) are interrelated and equally important. What happens in one domain affects the others, and all must be taken into account when practitioners create curricula that value the well-being and success of each individual child.

• Understanding human development is important, as the sequence of milestones is predictable and influences skill building. Practitioners must be familiar with the sequence in order to inform curriculum development and best practice in teaching.

• Children learn at different rates and at uneven rates within individual functioning, making high expectation and personalized learning necessary.

• Development and learning result from a constant push-pull of "biological maturation" (NAEYC, 2009a, n.p.) and childhood experiences, making it necessary for educators to be creative in providing experiences to children in which they can succeed.

• There are optimal periods in a child's life when individual experiences are more powerful and have a profound cumulative impact; thus, it is vital that children be supported during each learning and development activity.

• Child development, by its very nature, moves toward greater complexity in every domain, which means infants move from dependence and needing assistance to be soothed to toddlers and preschoolers who are able to self-regulate and manage their own emotions.

• Nurturing relationships with both adults and peers provide the best circumstances for development of key areas such as language and communication, empathy, self-regulation, cooperation, and much more.

• A multiple of social and cultural contexts influence development and learning, and exposure to a wide array of contexts is best for young children.

• A plethora of teaching strategies and a variety of interactions support learning and teaching of young children and should be used in combinations that are best for each child.

• Children who are challenged just beyond their current levels of mastery develop and learn best. Offering opportunities to practice new skills ensures that the new learning becomes ingrained and then new mastery tasks can take place. This continuum of learning takes place throughout life.

• Experiences influence children's motivation, persistence, initiative, and flexibility, and conversely, behaviors and dispositions influence the outcome of experiences.

• Self-regulation, the development of cognition, language, and social competence are learned through rich play experiences.

These twelve principles of child development inform a teacher practice that is developmentally appropriate in nature; however, NAEYC also has five guidelines that will help practitioners make important decisions and improve their practice. These are "(1) creating a caring community of learners, (2) teaching to enhance development and learning, (3) planning curriculum to achieve important goals, (4) assessing children's development and learning, and (5) establishing reciprocal relationships with families" (NAEYC, 2009a, n.p.).

Dual-Language Learners

The number of dual-language learners has recently exploded, requiring early-childhood professionals to re-examine their practices. Young children have a right to be assessed in their natural language, using cultural and linguistic cues that support their current understanding (NAEYC, 2009d). As a result, a set of seven recommendations has been drawn up by NAEYC to provide assessment that is appropriate and fair. For all students, these include the following:

- Screening and assessment must be used appropriately.
- Linguistic and cultural assessments must be appropriate to the child.
- Multiple professionals should assess the student and review data collectively.
- Formal assessments should be standardized.
- Those conducting the assessments should be bilingual, understand language acquisition, and understand the tool to be used.
- Include families in the assessment and decision-making process.
- Ensure that contributions are made to the field in order to develop better assessments and professional development opportunities (NAEYC, 2009d).

Early-Learning Standards

Defining the desired learning outcomes for infants, toddlers, and preschoolers is important, as they provide a framework for teaching and ensuring young children meet milestones. NAEYC uses a series of four elements to describe how early learning sets the stage for success and includes standards that (1) include developmentally appropriate content and outcomes, (2) are developed and reviewed using an inclusive process, (3) are implemented and assessed specifically to support the development of young children, and (4) support programs, professionals, and families whose focus is specific to young children (NAEYC, 2009c).

Perhaps of most significance is that all learning standards should be developmentally appropriate to the age of the child, taking into account cultural and personal characteristics as well as abilities and disabilities in children (NAEYC, 2009c). These standards are not scaled-back versions of standards used for school-age children, but rather include specific goals that directly affect the language, cognitive, social, and emotional spheres of young children (NAEYC, 2009c).

Through variety of research-based sources, as well as a wide selection of stakeholders, the learning standards are created and reviewed on a periodic basis (NAEYC, 2009c). They must be reviewed regularly to ensure that they "remain relevant and evidence-based" (NAEYC, 2009b, n.p.). These standards must be implemented and assessed to support the appropriate development of infants, toddlers, preschoolers, and children up to eight years of age. To do this, classroom practices and teaching strategies should support and promote learning, while the use of valid assessment instruments are needed to provide information that can be used to improve practice (NAEYC, 2009c).

Supporting children, families, and professionals is the last element of the learning standards. The emphasis here is placed on ensuring partnerships between families and the early-childhood program, as well as professional development for the staff of the program (NAEYC, 2009c). When used together, these four elements provide the basis for creating a set of exceptional standards that raise the bar for early childhood learning.

Standards for Professional Preparation

Practitioner standards are important in that they provide the expectations needed for professionals in the field of early-childhood education. NAEYC describes a collection of six standards that together focus on what "early childhood professionals should know and do, define essential learning outcomes in professional preparation programs and present a shared vision of excellence" (NAEYC, 2009e, n.p.). The standards require the application of skills and knowledge and expect early childhood educators to engage in a continuous cycle of "theory, research, and practice" (NAEYC, 2009e, n.p.).

When examined singly, the six standards describe different functions of a well-rounded professional. They include:

• Promoting child development and learning grounded in theory, and understanding the specific needs of children, as well as creating environments where children can thrive.
• Building family and community partnerships in which the value of the relationship is understood, and the reciprocal nature of each relationship empowers families and the community to be involved in the development of each child.
• Professionals not only know the importance of using a variety of assessment tools, but also sharing observation, assessment, and documentation collected regarding each child with families and professionals in order to positively influence growth and development.

- The use of developmentally appropriate practices, instructional strategies, and tools supports young children and influences their development and learning.
- Professionals build content knowledge in academic and developmental domains using appropriate resources and lesson planning to support and encourage learning in young children.
- Professional standards encourage educators to be collaborative, continuous learners who are reflective in nature and use what they learn to further best practice and policies for children and the field of early childhood education.

Accreditation

NAEYC is also known as an accrediting body for early-learning and early-childhood programs in higher education, and recognizes high-quality degree programs (NAEYC, n.d.). Each has its own requirements and standards, but all share a desire for high-performing, well-run programs. Through a self-study framework, external evaluation, and improvement in low-ranking areas, NAEYC-accredited programs are considered the gold standard in early care and education of both young children and adults (NAEYC, n.d.). Of note, early-childhood programs top 60,000 members, while NAEYC teacher-prep programs boast just shy of 200 accredited programs and more than 250 recognized programs (NAEYC, n.d.).

In total, the National Association for the Education of Young Children offers a comprehensive system for accreditation of programs for young children and adults, while offering position papers and research on topics vital to early childhood, young-child development, and public policy. The association offers annual conferences and professional development opportunities as well. The association boasts that it is the "largest and most important early childhood association" (NAEYC, n.d., n.p.), and with good reason.

FINAL THOUGHTS

Beginning in the 1960s with Lyndon B. Johnson's signing of the Elementary and Secondary Education Act through the modern-day Every Student Succeeds Act, early education and care has played a role in ensuring young children have access to quality education (Klein, 2016). Originally only for children of low-income families, preschool became the safe haven for all children, especially those with disabilities, dual-language learners, and those who were homeless or in foster care. Sadly, in 2014, not even half of all children ages three and four in the United States had access to high-quality, public, free day care (Barnett et al., 2015).

Using systems such as Head Start, QRIS, and NAEYC to ensure high-quality preschool and day care for all infants, toddlers, and preschoolers regardless of ability, financial state, housing, or language should increase the benefit to all young children and increase the chance for them to enter kindergarten on par with peers.

POINTS TO REMEMBER

- *IDEA Part B offers equal education to all young children, while Part C ensures services with measurable outcomes to young children with disabilities, both meant to prepare infants, toddlers, and preschoolers for the rigors of elementary school.*
- *A plethora of research studies indicate the importance of high-quality preschool for children of low-income families, those with disabilities, dual-language learners, and those who are homeless or in foster care.*
- *Head Start began in 1965 as a half-day/part-year program that serviced 561,000 children and has grown to be a model for educating young children and their families in the United States, with more than 927,000 children served in 2014 (ACF, 2017a).*
- *QRIS is a standards-based rating system used to rank childcare facilities and preschools. The ranking system assesses, improves, and communicates the levels of preschools and care facilities as a means to improve the overall quality of programs.*
- *The National Association for the Education of Young Children is an association committed to high-quality preschool and childcare. Accreditation of preschools, colleges, and recognized programs, professional development, conferences, and position papers are hallmarks of the NAEYC.*

Chapter 2

Identifying Children with Educational Needs and the Systems to Support Them

Typical infants, toddlers, and preschoolers grow and meet developmental milestones on a regular basis beginning at birth. However, atypical peers, those with disabilities or developmental delays, do not. For these children, it is vital that parents, doctors, caregivers, teachers, and practitioners recognize these delays and quickly get assistance. With the federally mandated Child Find system, children with suspected disabilities or developmental delays can be evaluated and, if found eligible, given the proper services that should help them make substantial gains in their areas of deficit.

Early intervention, or EI, is a system of coordinated services that helps families whose infants or toddlers are not meeting expected milestones (Center for Parent Information and Resources, 2014). Each family is provided with a service coordinator that supports them and helps them to understand the system. EI provides assistance and guidance during stressful times, allowing the family to be present and focused on the child. EI is family centered by design and purposefully includes all members in the evaluation of the infant or toddler, creation of the plan, and administration of services and interventions (Center for Parent Information and Resources, 2014). A cyclical process, families and providers come together often to assess child outcomes, tweak or change services, and make new decisions in the best interest of the child.

The Individualized Family Service Plan, or IFSP, is the mechanism that maintains all services, how often they will occur, their duration, and location for children ages birth to three years old. The preferred location is considered to be the natural environment, as it is felt that children learn best when they feel comfortable in their setting. Often, the natural environment is the child's home or a childcare setting in which the child is enrolled, ensuring that family considerations and challenges are acknowledged; incidentally, this often helps all constituents to participate in this process.

For some families, learning that their child has a disability can be life altering. To assist them, there are a variety of services and people to help them come to terms with this new way of living. Parents and caregivers move through a series of emotions as they try to understand what has happened and what to do next for their child (Eichenstein, 2015). Under such circumstances, it may not be an easy process and as such, families are advised to work together with a variety of service providers who can assist them. All of these factors create a template meant to support both the family and the child as they work toward more positive developmental outcomes.

CHILD FIND

IDEA Part C includes a mandate called Child Find (Wright and Wright, 2016). This mandate states that public school districts are required to "identify, locate, and evaluate all children with disabilities" (Wright and Wright, 2016, n.p.), regardless of the severity. This mandate applies to all children from birth to age twenty-one, regardless of state, school of choice, migrant or homeless status, or status as a ward of the state. It also includes children who maintain passing grades despite having a suspected disability. Finding children early may help decrease services over time so it is essential to locate children as young as possible.

There are seven specific elements included in a Child Find program. These include: (1) defining the target population, (2) raising public awareness, (3) referral and intake of a child referred for services, (4) screening and identification of a child who may have a disability or a developmental delay, (5) eligibility determination, (6) tracking children who receive services, and (7) interagency coordination for states in which multiple agencies share resources (Special Education Guide, 2017a). It is important to use the Child Find program, as it delineates what is federally mandated and ensures children are assessed and given proper services.

A parent, caregiver, pediatrician, practitioner, teacher, or other professional may choose to refer a child for early intervention through Child Find. This is usually initiated when a child has not met a milestone or a significant deficit is noticed. Once contacted, the early intervention agency has two days to either refer or decline the child for evaluation (Special Education Guide, 2017b). Either Child Find or the early intervention program will assign the parent a service coordinator. This person is responsible for guiding the family through each step of the evaluation and identification process.

According to IDEA Part C, parents must be informed about the process and any possible actions that may be taken. This is called "prior written notice," and the purpose is to ensure that parents are completely informed and aware of the actions to be taken on behalf of the child (Center for Parent Information and Resources, 2012). The information must be presented in the family's native language, written in a way that is easy to read, and an interpreter should be present to help families understand the requirements and ask questions.

In addition to prior written notice, parental consent must be given for any and all changes to take place or services to be rendered (Center for Parent Information and Resources, 2012). IDEA Part C requires that this be in writing, in the family's native language, and that consent must be given voluntarily and can be revoked at any time (Center for Parent Information and Resources, 2012). Both prior written notice and parental consent are required three times during the evaluation process: before screenings are given, before conducting the evaluation, and before assessments (Center for Parent Information and Resources, 2012).

CHILD EVALUATION

Once written consent from the parent has been obtained by the service coordinator or case manager, screenings and evaluations can be completed. Each screening or evaluation is completed by a certified or licensed professional with expertise in the respective area of concern (Center for Parent Information and Resources, 2014). In addition, the parents will be asked to complete paperwork and observe their child by using a survey, taking notes, or both (Center for Parent Information and Resources, 2014).

Using the five domains of early childhood development as checkpoints, the child will be evaluated to see if he or she is indeed in need of services (Fleming, 2015). These five domains—physical, social, cognitive, language, and adaptation—are important features when determining ability. Once mastered, each area helps the student flourish, and conversely, when one component is incomplete, the child suffers, making EI services necessary.

Physical development is the most visible of the milestones. It includes the mastering of balance and fine and gross motor skills—all things movement. As children grow from infant to toddler to preschooler, parents watch them become independent: first rolling over, then sitting up, crawling, standing, taking their first steps, and finally walking confidently (Aiger, 2017). Motor skills are also quickly established as the child learns to build with blocks, picking them up and moving them from place to place, using scissors, and drawing circles, lines, and eventually people.

Making and maintaining relationships is considered social development. Toddlers begin with parallel play and, as they move to the preschool stage, soon master cooperative play and conflict resolution. Young children will tend to show off their abilities, yet they can be very empathetic toward others (Aiger, 2017). Other milestones within this development area include group games and fair play, and although they know the difference between reality and fantasy, they are able to play imaginatively with peers and siblings (Spivey, 2017).

Thinking and knowing are within the domain of cognitive development (Spivey, 2017). Here, sorting and organizing by attributes is one of the first jobs for a child. "How" and "when" questions follow as the brain further develops, and an understanding of counting, colors, and name recognition are included in the preschool years (Aiger, 2017). Understanding the difference between fact and fiction or truth and lies is yet another milestone that must be accomplished during this time period.

Language development is the ability to understand the spoken word as well as using verbal expression to be understood (Aiger, 2017). Whereas toddlers say only a few words at a time, preschoolers have mastered full sentences and positional words (Spivey, 2017). Additional milestones include sharing personal information and experiences and conversing clearly with peers and adults.

Adaptive skills make up the fifth domain to be examined through testing and surveys and refer to the ability to take care of oneself to a certain degree. Daily living skills such as eating, dressing, toileting, and washing are at the heart of this domain (Aiger, 2017). As infants, children are dependent on the family for support; however, as they move from toddler to preschooler, their level of independence increases, and their ability to use utensils, pour items from a container, and use snaps and buttons becomes more precise.

Once all the information about the child in question has been collected, it is the responsibility of the team to gather and review each individual survey or evaluation. If the team decides the child is in need of early intervention services for children under the age of three, they move to create an Individualized Family Service Plan (Center for Parent Information and Resources, 2016). A precursor to the Individualized Education Plan (IEP) used for children three and older, the IFSP is a federally mandated document that clearly details what a child with a disability needs in services and includes the family as an integral part of the plan.

UNDERSTANDING AN INDIVIDUALIZED
FAMILY SERVICE PLAN

A child from birth to the age of three who has a documented disability or developmental delay qualifies for early intervention services, and an IFSP is created. This document describes how the child is functioning at the time of assessment, outlines specific needs to be addressed, and concludes with expected outcomes (Center for Parent Information and Resources, 2016). The treatment plan details all services the child with disabilities is entitled to under the law and, additionally, outlines the location, duration, and any other specifics needed. The IFSP places a premium on families, that is, how to support them so they can best support the child; therefore, it is created based on detailed input from the family (Special Education Guide, 2017c).

The IFSP is developed by a complex team, whose members are all committed to the success of the child, and while the specific members involved in the creation of the IFSP will vary depending on the early intervention needs, the team always begins with the family. It is the family who knows the child best. It will also comprise any number of the following: a family advocate and/or service coordinator from the EI program, a pediatrician, a psychiatrist, an occupational or physical therapist, a neurologist or speech-language pathologist, and/or any number of other professionals who can directly influence student outcomes (Special Education Guide, 2017a).

Once it has been determined that the child is eligible for services, the team has thirty days to write the plan and have it signed by the parents. Before that can occur, the team must examine the testing completed and seek answers from the family about routines, child preferences and challenges, as well as their hopes, dreams, goals, and outcomes for the child (Special Education Guide, 2017c). As this process is family centered, it is vital that the family communicate issues such as transportation difficulties, day care needs, or need for training to understand the disability or specific caregiver interventions (U.S. Department of Justice, 2017; Center for Parent Information and Resources, 2016). All of these factors will assist in writing goals and creating a document that will be beneficial to the child.

The parent has the difficult job of maintaining comprehensive records that will help the team. This must begin early in the EI process and should include copies of tests, notes from therapists or doctors, and anything else that might help create a more specific IFSP. Families who ask for written copies of requested or suggested therapies or services stand a better chance of having those items included in the IFSP. Parents often come to meetings with large binders filled with items like these (Special Education Guide, 2017c). Being prepared is good practice, and it is also a time-saver.

COMPONENTS OF THE INDIVIDUALIZED FAMILY SERVICE PLAN

Although each state has some latitude regarding regulations and procedures, some components are federally mandated, as outlined in IDEA, Part C (n.d.).

These components can be found within the document, which is usually pre-formed and requires the team to fill in the blanks or write short answers. They include writing down (1) the name of the early intervention coordinator and the organizations involved in servicing the child, (2) current level of functioning, (3) pertinent information about the family, (4) specific interventions and services to be put in place, and (5) desired outcomes (Center for Parent Information and Resources, 2016; Special Education Guide, 2017c).

Providers list. This section of the IFSP must include the name of the early intervention service coordinator who will work directly with the family. It is also customary to include the service providers and organizations/individuals who are responsible for paying for all the interventions to be implemented (Special Education Guide, 2017c).

Current level of functioning. This section defines what the child is capable of doing prior to inception of services and interventions. The results from current testing may be included here, such as cognitive and psychological testing; hearing and vision tests; speech, occupational, or physical therapy evaluations or screenings; as well as pediatrician or psychiatrist notes and surveys or notes from the family regarding social development (Center for Parent Information and Resources, 2016)

Pertinent family information. In this case, the more information the family is able to provide, the better, as it helps the team understand the needs of the child and household. Considerations include prenatal care and birth experiences, post-birth conditions, members of the extended family and the role they play within the family dynamics, and the strengths, concerns, and priorities of the family unit (Special Education Guide, 2017c).

Interventions and services. This section details what the services and interventions are, who will administer them, and the duration and location of each, although EI most often occurs in the natural setting, usually the home or the childcare setting. For example, if "Mary" has weak muscle tone in her hands and cannot grasp and hold small items, the IFSP might state that she will meet with an occupational therapist for three one-hour sessions each week (Center for Parent Information and Resources, 2016).

Desired outcomes. A critical component of the IFSP, outcomes must be specific, relevant, and measurable. An example of a well-written goal might be: "Mary will grasp a block, raise it up, and move it from one container to the other in nine out of ten attempts." These short-term goals are reviewed by the team every six months. At these meetings, it will be determined if the child has met the goal, needs more time with the goal, or needs the goal tweaked or changed completely (Special Education Guide, 2017c).

Once the IFSP is signed, services can begin. Providers most often come to the home, although at times it is decided that a specific location is a better fit for various reasons: for example, going to the park to practice running because the child lives in an apartment with no useable space outside. Providers need to remember that parents can elect not to participate in services and may revoke the services at any time (Center for Parent Information and Resources, 2016).

INDIVIDUALIZED EDUCATION PLAN

Once a child turns three years old, he or she no longer qualifies for an IFSP and, if services are still warranted, must instead be placed on an Individualized Education Plan. The difference between the two plans is simple: an IFSP focuses on coordinating services that help the family enhance developmental outcomes for the child, while an IEP meets the needs of a student in an academic setting (Center for Parent Information and Resources, 2014; Podvey, Hinojosa, and Koenig, 2013).

There are other differences as well. An IFSP is reviewed every six months, whereas an IEP is reviewed annually, and full testing is done every three years. In an IFSP, the statement of performance gives the child's present developmental levels of functioning in the social-emotional domain, communication and cognitive domains, and the area of self-help; however, an IEP is focused on the present level of academic achievement and functional performance levels (Center for Parent Information and Resources, 2014).

Services are rendered in a natural setting in an IFSP, whereas an IEP is written so that students are able to show progress in the least restrictive general education setting, with either modifications or supports and services, and with both able-bodied and atypical students (United Cerebral Palsy, 2017b). An IFSP calls for outcomes and activities to be specific to the needs of the child and family, while in an IEP, the goals and measurable objectives are written expressly to address the academic needs of the student (Podvey et al., 2013; United Cerebral Palsy, 2017a).

These differences are important, as the two plans serve different purposes. The IFSP is meant to address the youngest children and help them reach developmental milestones. An IEP focuses on creating a learning environment where typical and disabled peers have opportunities to learn in the same environment with the same curriculum, using modifications and assistive technologies to provide a level playing field.

UNDERSTANDING PARENTAL EMOTIONS

Perhaps the most difficult thing for a parent to hear is that their child is not typical. A typical infant, toddler, or preschooler will meet and successfully manage developmental milestones in the appropriate time frame, while atypical peers may not. For the parents of these children, reframing their thoughts and life plans often takes substantial time and effort (Eichenstein, 2015). There are five stages that most parents and extended families experience when they receive the news about their child having a disability, although it is interesting to note that the stages may occur at the same time, in sequence, or not at all, and that different members may be in different stages at the same time (Eichenstein, 2015).

The stages include denial/retreat, anger/aggression, bargaining/control/ solutions, depression/shame, and acceptance/integration (Eichenstein, 2015). *Denial* is a natural first response, as parents may go into shock when they hear the news; however, as soon as they can emotionally handle it, parents should get a second opinion and find an expert to help (Eichenstein, 2015).

The next stage is *anger/aggression*. Here, denial has worn off, and reality is difficult to accept. The truth is often painful, and, as such, it may be replaced with anger (Eichenstein, 2015).

In the third stage, family members try to *bargain* as a way to gain control over a situation they ultimately cannot control. Some might look excessively on the internet for obscure solutions; however, it is better to suggest that they assemble a team of professionals to support the child (Eichenstein, 2015).

Stage four ushers in *depression*. Families are afraid, stressed, and trying to figure out if their child will ever be okay. They are also wondering if the disability is their fault, if somehow they could have prevented it. Professionals should advise families to find a support system of others like them who can share experiences and offer understanding (Eichenstein, 2015).

The final stage is *acceptance*, and it is hard won. Once here, parents are able to advocate for their child, offer solace to other families, and sometimes find new meaning in tasks. The realization and acceptance of a family that their child has a disability or developmental delay is not a closed door, but rather a starting point of a new process, a different way of thinking and being (Eichenstein, 2015). Acceptance is helpful for families in that they are able to see the positive and envision a future of possibilities.

MODIFYING THE HOME TO ACCOMMODATE THE DIAGNOSED CHILD

For some children who have been diagnosed with a disability, providing outside services and interventions is not enough or is not appropriate. For these cases, the best approach is to prepare the house so the child can be comfortable and experience success with everyday tasks. This may include home modifications, assistive technology, and mobility and visual supports, among other things. In each case, the outcome should add value to the child's daily life.

Home Modifications

Home modifications are especially important for a child in a wheelchair or a young child with vision or hearing loss. In these cases, it is important to make sure, if possible, that the house is on one level with no steps or abrupt floor changes. The doorways should be at least thirty-six inches wide and hallways should be forty-two inches wide (United Cerebral Palsy, 2017a). In the bathroom, there should be grab bars, a chair-height toilet, and a roll-under sink, among other modifications. Everything needs to be easily accessible.

Assistive Technology

Assistive technology is any device that helps a person with a disability do "better than s/he can do without the device" (Reed, 2017, n.p.). It can be as simple as a light switch that is modified to allow for a wheelchair-bound child to be independent, or a pencil grip, sound system, or clipboard (Reed, 2017). It can also be as complex as a laptop or communication device. Most often, it is easier to think about what technology is not: it is not a person, strategy, method, or assignment modification (Reed, 2017). Assistive technology is a multitude of different actions meant to help a child accomplish a task.

Visual Supports

A visual support is anything that helps an individual get through the day, from a sign to designate the bathroom to a list of homework assignments. Visual supports help people stay on task, communicate, and express themselves (Alder, Rosenfeld, and Procter, 2017). Nonverbal children may use gestures, facial expressions, or speech-generated devices (Alder et al., 2017). Schedules can be made using pictures instead of words, for children who have yet to master the written word. The list is long, and supports that will help a child who is disabled in this way are abundant.

Importance of Service Providers

Service providers, including occupational therapists, physical therapists, and speech-language pathologists, are important members of the IFSP and IEP delivery system and cannot be overlooked. These valuable team members are the backbone of change, as they work directly with the children and families to provide services and learning accommodations for infants, toddlers, and preschoolers who have been diagnosed with developmental delays (Opp, 2017). According to IDEA, these services should be given in the natural setting, or the one in which the child is most comfortable, whenever possible.

Occupational therapists (OTs), physical therapists (PTs), and speech and language pathologists (S-LPs) play an important part in helping infants, toddlers, preschoolers, and their families make progress when a developmental delay is identified in one of those areas. Occupational therapists deal with typical living activities, physical therapists look at motor skills, and S-LPs are concerned with speech and language disorders (American Occupational Therapy Association, 2017a; American Physical Therapy Association, 2017; Speech-Language & Audiology Canada, 2017)

Occupational therapists. An occupational therapist is interested in helping to improve daily activities, using research-based interventions and strategies. A child's life is made up of a series of activities, or occupations, including, but not limited to, sleeping, playing and interacting with others, getting dressed, and other daily activities (American Occupational Therapy Association, 2017b). The end goal is always independence; however, this may involve modifying some activities to make them achievable.

Infants who experience problems with fine motor skills as well as cognitive or sensory processing, may need the assistance of an OT (Birth Injury Guide, 2017a). An infant who has fine motor skill deficits such as muscle tone, dexterity, and hyper- or hyposensitivity may receive help such as physical development exercises, muscle strengthening training, and toy stimulation (Birth Injury Guide, 2017a). Once these goals are achieved, the OT will work toward the child's holding a bottle, spoon, or other self-care skills (Birth Injury Guide, 2017a).

Sensory integration, or sensory processing, describes the way the nervous system takes in and makes sense of messages and then responds. Here, the issue is an unusual sensitivity to touch that results in infants having a difficult time with touch, light, or sound. The OT will develop a plan to increase touch, sound, or light accordingly to help the baby. Some interventions include specialized toys and activities, sand and water therapy, vestibular therapies, and more (Birth Injury Guide, 2017a).

Physical therapists. Infants, toddlers, and preschoolers who may have disorders or disabilities that affect their balance, muscle control, or attaining milestones, or those who have trouble moving properly, will see a PT for services, once they are diagnosed (Birth Injury Guide, 2017b). Some such disabilities or disorders might include cerebral palsy, autism, neuromuscular disorders, and more (Birth Injury Guide, 2017b).

Physical therapists work with the infant, toddler, or preschooler and the family to ensure independence. For babies born prematurely, PTs give therapies to help maintain proper posture; this is accomplished through specific exercises and massages (Birth Injury Guide, 2017b). Other therapies may include developing age-appropriate skills, improving muscle function, and targeting movement patterns and posture (Birth Injury Guide, 2017b). Not only do the physical therapists do the work, but they show the families how to as well so these small children can receive additional help even when the PT is not there.

Speech and language pathologists. S-LPs treat a wide range of developmental delays in young children, including swallowing and feeding disorders, pre-literacy and literacy skills, cognitive-communication disorders, language delays and disorders, speech delays and disorders, and fluency issues (Speech-Language & Audiology Canada, 2017).

In infants, S-LPs work to improve feeding abilities and develop communication skills that may be lacking (Birth Injury Guide, 2017c). There are a number of signs that may indicate a problem, including coughing or gagging during feedings, frequent spitting up, and poor weight gain or growth. Therapies include oral stimulation, feeding interventions, and the promotion of early speech through specific activities.

Toddlers and preschoolers with speech problems may benefit from therapies specific to their problems, such as articulation, fluency, resonance, or voice issues (Birth Injury Guide, 2017c; Patino, 2017). When toddlers and preschoolers have trouble with receptive and expressive language or pragmatic language skills, an S-LP will develop a protocol for helping the child.

All providers work with the child and the family in combination to produce the best results. While IDEA suggests that this be accomplished in a natural setting such as the home, time may also be spent in a facility that is specific to the disability, such as a physical therapy center. Childcare centers or preschools are also common locations for intervention services to occur (Patino, 2017).

Therapists, S-LPs, and other interventionists who see atypical children in childcare centers or preschools are able to help them be successful in real-world settings. They are able to improve fine and gross motor skills as they apply to things that happen within the course of the child's day, as well as provide specialized academic activities. Children who use assistive devices for cognitive and physical challenges can be evaluated and helped. S-LPs can assist students with swallowing and food challenges, as well as with a variety of speech and language issues (Speech-Language & Audiology Canada, 2017).

FINAL THOUGHTS

The process of finding atypical children is completed through Child Find. This federally mandated program specifically seeks out children with disabilities who may be entitled to special education services. Infants and toddlers with disabilities or developmental delays are serviced through early intervention, which coordinates evaluations and services that are created in an Individualized Family Service Plan.

The EI service coordinator, family, doctors, and team members are responsible for writing the IFSP and ensuring that the five components are specifically stated. This ensures that the plan is accurate and contains all vital information required to execute the plan. From the name of the early intervention coordinator and the organizations involved in servicing the child, the current level of function, and pertinent information about the family, to the specific services needed and the desired outcomes, the IFSP is a very involved and detailed plan meant to improve child outcomes and, hopefully, spare the child additional time in special education later on in life.

As a child turns three, it is time to replace the IFSP with the Individualized Education Plan so that appropriate actions can be taken at preschool and beyond. If an educator sees a problem with a child who has not had early intervention services, he or she may request an evaluation. Similar to an IFSP, the IEP process involves evaluation and a team meeting to decide on necessary interventions. Parents must sign off on several steps of the process.

When families find out there is a disability, an abundance of emotions take over. Working through them takes time and patience. Denial is the first emotion, followed by anger and bargaining. Depression is the fourth stage, and once through that dark place, family members arrive at acceptance, which allows advocacy to take place. Some family members will find themselves in different stages during the process, and some members will not experience all the stages.

Children with disabilities may need accommodations made to their home. Opening doorways and adding features that are compliant with the Americans with Disabilities Act will ensure the child is able to be as independent as possible (Alder et al., 2017). Using visual supports is important for the child who may want to communicate but has previously been unable to. Communication devices, schedules, and other visuals also help with this. When the goal is independence, there is no limit to the creativity available.

Occupational and physical therapists and speech-language pathologists are but a few of the interventionists available to help atypical children navigate and successfully master skills not in their repertoire. Together with family support, the team works to ensure that the skills are transferrable to all areas of life and school.

POINTS TO REMEMBER

• *Child Find is federally mandated in IDEA Part C as a way to ensure that all children with disabilities and developmental delays are found and that services are provided as early as possible, as a way to, hopefully, shorten the need for continued support later in life.*

- *Early intervention is a system of federally mandated services for young children, birth to age three, who have diagnosed disabilities or developmental delays. It is designed to use interventions to help infants and toddlers meet milestones to increase their chances for success and decrease their need for special education services as they get older.*
- *An Individualized Family Service Plan (IFSP) is a roadmap that includes early intervention services and supports the family and atypical child. Based on current levels of functioning and projected outcomes, interventions and support are put into place with parental consent.*
- *An Individualized Education Plan (IEP) is the next iteration of an IFSP and begins at age three. The IEP process is similar to the IFSP process in that it involves evaluation, team meetings, and planned outcomes. For children who have been on an IFSP or who are newly diagnosed, the IEP offers a plan of action including current levels of functioning, developmental and educational gaps, service providers, timing, and goals for success.*
- *The five emotional stages parents often face when told they have an atypical child include denial, anger, bargaining, depression, and acceptance. Each family member will move through the stages differently, or not at all. Once at acceptance, however, the real work can begin, positivity will rule, and advocacy is possible.*
- *Setting up the home for the child who is disabled will look different depending on the needs of the individual. It may be opening doorways and leveling floors, or it may be visual supports and communication devices. Either way, it is the best interest of the child that must guide the changes to be made.*

Chapter 3

Childhood Development

Influences from the Outside In

Children with disabilities, ages five and under, account for 1 percent of the disabled population in the United States (Kraus, 2017). The Centers for Disease Control (CDC) (2015) reports that approximately "15% of children aged 3–17 years have one or more developmental disabilities" (n.p.). That translates into a ratio of one in six children born with or who will develop special learning needs requiring some type of service. These are often found when children do not reach normal developmental milestones such as learning to walk, talk, play, or behave (CDC, 2015).

According to UNICEF (2013), children with disabilities are discriminated against for a number of reasons, making them "one of the most marginalized groups" (p. 4). Some infants are born into undesirable geographical locations, suffer from poverty, or face dietary issues (Pem, 2015). Adults may lack the proper understanding of the parental role, exhibiting a variety of parenting styles and/or behaviors that might affect child development (Allen and Kelly, 2015). Emotional stability in the home as well as external socialization cannot be overlooked as factors that influence growth in young children.

Allen and Kelly (2015) posit that the first thousand days of life set the stage for optimal health, improved cognition, and higher learning capacity. Infants, toddlers, and preschoolers are in the hands of the adults around them to support, guide, and nurture them through the first years of life. For some children, this is an easy process filled with warmth, comfort, and guidance. For others, the stresses that surround them prove to be daunting, overwhelming, and life altering. There are numerous developmental challenges faced by this youngest population that they cannot control and that will affect the remainder of their lives.

GEOGRAPHICAL AND ENVIRONMENTAL CONSIDERATIONS

Geographical considerations determine the quality of housing basics such as water and indoor plumbing, power, and the conditions found in the neighborhoods surrounding the family (UNICEF, 2013). Families who live in geographically undesirable locations may find it is difficult to raise children with disabilities due to the terrain surrounding the house and/or neighborhood.

Environmental concerns include lead or mercury exposure, poor drinking water, salmonella, and inadequate sanitation (Pem, 2015; UNICEF, 2013). Children born into such conditions are more likely to show developmental disabilities over time and, once identified, receive less care and fewer resources; thus, they become more disabled (UNICEF, 2013).

Children who are in families where there is little eye contact, where children do not develop bonds with caring adults, and who do not have opportunities to explore and play may be at greater risk to be developmentally delayed. Children who are born with sensory challenges that are not addressed while the child is young most likely will develop more problems that may take longer to resolve.

POVERTY AND DIETARY CONSIDERATIONS

Globally, more than two hundred million children under five are affected by poor health, malnutrition, lack of health care, and poverty (Pem, 2015; UNICEF, 2013). Due to these issues, cognitive and social development may be stunted and, often, their potentials never met (Allen and Kelly, 2015). Where infants, toddlers, and preschoolers are born, the circumstances surrounding familial poverty as well as dietary concerns are out of their control yet set the stage for future growth and learning.

Families in poverty may move from shelter to shelter and not be able to provide consistency, clean clothing, and food. Dietary concerns include the need to provide healthy and high-quality food options for infants and young children, which in turn help their bodies and brains grow properly (Pem, 2015). Dietary concerns and poverty contribute in part or in whole to infant, toddler, and preschool child impairments that can be apparent at birth or can surface years after (UNICEF, 2013).

Poverty

In the United States, 11.4 million children under the age of five live in poverty, while another 5.9 million live just above the poverty line (Jiang, Ekono, and Skinner, 2014). According to current research, households that include a disabled person are more likely to experience poverty and have fewer assets (UNICEF, 2013; World Health Organization [WHO], 2011). This directly impacts children with disabilities, as they are more likely to be deprived of basic necessities as the family struggles to provide the medically or physically necessary items.

Children with disabilities who live in poverty are more likely to drop out of school prior to graduation (Doar and Wassink, 2015). Many are being raised by a single parent and/or have a parent who is not employed, while others may live in a household where another member is disabled and receives benefits (Doar and Wassink, 2015; WHO, 2012). It is important, therefore, to examine ways to improve outcomes for these children.

Dietary Considerations

Due to the high number of infants, toddlers, and preschoolers with disabilities who live in poverty, it is not surprising that they might be the same children who suffer from a lack of quality food choices (WHO, 2012). It is important, then, that caregivers receive coaching in purchasing high-quality fruits and vegetables, meats, and milk. Some families have state or federal assistance and, if so, must buy only certain foods with that money.

For infants, breastmilk provides the best combination of natural ingredients for optimal growth and development; however, high-quality formula is also an option. Complementary feeding of meats, fruits, and vegetables beginning at six months of age provides the next set of nutritional needs for infants and toddlers but does not replace the need for breastmilk and/or nutritious formula. This combination is most likely to prevent initial malnutrition and developmental delays (Pem, 2015).

All children are entitled to a free, federally subsidized meal program, assuming they live in poverty or low-income homes. As this is often the case for children with disabilities, there are programs that cover private day care and preschool centers, as well as public schools (USDA Food and Nutrition Service, 2017a, b). For example, the National School Lunch Program (USDA Food and Nutrition Service, 2017b) served 30.4 million children in 2016.

These programs have compliance requirements to ensure meals and snacks are well balanced and healthy and meet strict federal requirements. The parents of toddlers and preschoolers, especially those with disabilities, who attend specialized programs may find these options available to them (USDA Food and Nutrition Service, 2017b).

HEALTH CARE

Access to basic health care may be lacking for those children born with disabilities or who become disabled due to external factors in some areas (UNICEF, 2013; WHO, 2012). Additional factors that limit health care include limited knowledge regarding what is needed and/or inability of the family to access health care.

Both attitudes and economic development can be triggers for such issues; however, in developed countries this is less of a concern, as morbidity and mortality rates of children with disabilities have decreased significantly (UNICEF, 2013). Ensuring that children have access to pediatricians and specialists who can diagnose and treat their specific issues is essential.

PARENTING CONSIDERATIONS

Infants, toddlers, and preschoolers are dependent on caregivers to ensure they are given the attention needed for optimal growth and development (Pem, 2015). Newborns have the potential to learn soon after birth, using their senses as activators. Play is the connector that provides opportunities for interaction and communication with caregivers; thus, it is vital that parents connect with and provide positive interactions for their child who has a disability (Pem, 2015). Reduced or nonexistent care substantially affects the development of cognitive capacity, growth, health, and personality (Pem, 2015). Accordingly, stress and adversity in early childhood increases the risk for learning disabilities and stress-related diseases (Pem, 2015).

Caregivers may treat the disabled youngster differently or may not spend quality time with the child, which can compromise interventions (WHO, 2012). Another factor to consider is a lack of information given to the parent or caregiver. If the primary contact with the child is not armed with information, there will be a struggle to support the child's needs. Providing guidance to the caregivers and family is critical and will ensure that the infant, toddler, or preschooler is given every opportunity to succeed.

Sadly, young children with disabilities are three to four times more likely than their able-bodied peers to experience neglect, violence, or sexual, physical, or psychological abuse in their own home, school, or care center (WHO, 2012). They become easy prey for family members and strangers alike, and this leads to feelings of powerlessness and low self-esteem (WHO, 2012). Social services, child protection, supports, and services are available for children with disabilities and their families, to ensure positive outcomes.

Family services aim to identify families needing services and then offer training, knowledge, and skills to meet the needs of the child with disabilities, not just in the home but across all settings (WHO, 2012). Here, it is important to also include extended family, as they play a supportive role in ensuring the child and family are on solid ground.

SOCIALIZATION

Social programs and services play a significant role in the socialization of children with disabilities. It is the responsibility of the caregiver and health team to find activities that the child can access and participate in (WHO, 2012). Activities such as play groups, library reading programs, gym groups, field trips, and preschool day care all serve different purposes.

Play Groups

Free play groups for preschool-aged children with disabilities and their families are offered in many communities (Bayada Home Health Care, 2017). These are places where children can play with peers in a safe environment while caregivers can connect and find support (Bayada Home Health Care, 2017). While the children are playing, parents are learning valuable skills in how to build their child's brain, support their physical development, and learn about better nutrition and community resources that are available for them to use (Mead, 2017). Other play groups are similar, although some offer facilitated play while caregivers attend support-group meetings and hear special guest speakers.

Library Reading Programs

The Wayland Free Public Library of Wayland, Massachusetts (2017), as well as other libraries across the country, offers Sensory Storytime, specifically for children with sensory integration issues, autism, or other developmental disabilities, as well as for typical peers. The site ensures caregivers that they are sensitive to the needs of these special populations, offering a visual schedule and mentioning that children's behaviors are tolerated.

Music Programs

Various music programs are available to support children with disabilities. Two such examples include a music studio in Sudbury, Massachusetts, as well as the Boston Conservatory. Both offer students who are gifted, struggling, or disabled, and as young as four years old, lessons that use multisensory strategies to engage the learner. The studio owner explains that by focusing on a variety of learning styles—auditory, visual, tactile, and kines-thetic—students have a more "concrete and complete learning experience" (Success Music Studio, n.d.).

Gym, Dance, Gymnastics, and Swim Programs

A variety of gyms, dance studios, and town recreation departments offer adaptive programming, specifically geared for young children and those with disabilities, meant to improve their quality of life.

Equine Therapy

The use of horses to help with emotional growth of children and adults with disabilities is not new. Horses respond and give feedback to the rider and are able to mimic the rider's emotion, making them extremely responsive to the needs of those with disabilities (Equestrian Therapy, 2017). This type of therapy can enhance the emotional, behavioral, physical, and cognitive skills of children and adults with disabilities (Equestrian Therapy, 2017).

For young children, equestrian therapy has been shown to increase speech, language, communication, motor skills, muscle tone, and coordination (Equestrian Therapy, 2017). Children with Asperger's syndrome, autism, and other learning disabilities also benefit from equine therapy. For these children, stimulation of several senses creates a safe space and encourages communication skills and physical contact (Equestrian Therapy, 2017).

Preschool

Preschool offers children with disabilities a first chance to explore and grow under the care of professionals. Public preschools follow Title I federal rules and must follow the Individualized Education Plan devised by the team, which includes teachers, therapists, special education staff, and family (U.S. Department of Education, 2012). Children are placed with typical peers as models, and trained staff use developmentally appropriate practices to teach the children. Those on IEPs receive additional help and accommodations in class, and the educator is required to complete quarterly progress reports for the parents (U.S. Department of Education, 2012).

FINAL THOUGHTS

Our youngest children grow rapidly during the first five years of life, espe-cially the first thousand days. Understanding the factors that affect child development and cognitive abilities may help prevent the need for special education services or, at the very least, reduce the number or scope of services needed. Infants, toddlers, and preschoolers with disabilities are one of the most marginalized groups and face many battles, many of which are beyond their control.

Geography and environment play a role in development after birth, as do the level of poverty and dietary concerns. Children who have disabilities face an additional uphill battle with parents who are sometimes unsure of how to help their child, as well as of correct parenting styles and behaviors. Abuse and neglect is more common in children with disabilities. All of these can be combatted with collaboration between caregivers and team members.

POINTS TO REMEMBER

- *Some disabilities are clearly seen at birth, while other delays are most often discovered when children miss important milestones.*
- *The first thousand days are the most critical as they set the stage for optimal health, improved cognition, and higher learning capacity.*
- *Geography and environmental concerns contribute, either positively or negatively, to child growth and development. Some children born into areas or homes with unsanitary water, lead, or mercury are exposed to pathogens and will become disabled over time.*
- *Disabled persons, especially children, are more likely to live in poverty. This leads to poor dietary conditions with limited healthy food options.*
- *Infants, toddlers, and preschoolers depend on caregivers to provide necessary comfort, attention, and communication. Reduced or nonexistent care substantially affects children who are disabled or who become disabled over time.*
- *Socialization is important to child development, especially for those who have a disability. Examples of socialization activities are swimming, music or dance classes, equestrian therapy, library reading groups, play groups, and preschool.*

Chapter 4

Home-School Partnerships
Connecting Where It Counts

Parents have the most influential role in the development of their child's academic achievement from birth to adulthood (Epstein, 2011; Hynes, 2014). In early childhood, parents are responsible for the development of children's cognitive and language skills, and they are also tasked with promoting literacy, which are all shown to have an impact on achievement. During middle and high school years, parental responsibility shifts to fostering educational socialization and preparing children for college and career achievement, which in totality encompasses the whole of family engagement throughout a child's academic career (Hynes, 2014; Office of the Education Ombudsman, 2012).

Family and school partnerships are not limited to parents' helping their children at home, but also include working with specialists such as faith-based or community programs, before- or after-school programs, or occupational, physical, medical, and academic interventions (Office of the Education Ombudsman, 2012). Parents are the determinant as to participation in community social and educational opportunities and must be cooperative with educators and practitioners (Drang, 2011).

Partnering with families ensures collaboration between home/caregivers and educators/practitioners for the purpose of increasing positive outcomes at school. This also applies to the developmental and educational success of our youngest population, those who are disabled, and most importantly, those who may be both disabled and under the age of five.

Several pundits (Epstein et al., 2002; Grant and Ray, 2016) agree that family engagement, or partnerships that include families and educators/practitioners, requires a strong connection and must be mutually collaborative. Although engagement ought to mean group decision making and working together, for some families it means just showing up at school for events, open houses, and conferences. Mapp (2014) discusses the importance of building capabilities. These skills and knowledge support engagement and strong families and include advocacy skills, language acquisition, building relationships where trust is the primary motivation, and cultural competency (Mapp, 2014; Mead, 2017).

It is incumbent on the knowledgeable stakeholders to provide ongoing and positive ways in which to engage with families. The community in which the family exists must nurture relationships and provide the tools that enable participation; thus, family-school partnerships have a multitude of facets that must be addressed in order for there to be attainable developmental and academic success for all children, especially infants, toddlers, and preschoolers who may have more specific needs.

NATURE AND IMPORTANCE OF
HOME-SCHOOL PARTNERSHIPS

Early childcare and education for families was mandated at the federal level in 1965 for families at or below the poverty line (K12 Academics, 2017). In more recent times, the Every Student Succeeds Act redefined partnering with families to include providing information in the families' native language, offering training and materials to assist in parenting skill building, providing reasonable accommodations to students when requested by parents, and educating staff, school leaders, and administration. Other updates include helping families to understand the education system and state-specific standards, in addition to coordinating state and federal programs to include preschool (Klein, 2016).

More recent studies, however, demonstrate that the greatest impact lies in the need for educator, practitioner, and family cooperation across all demographics as a way to influence positive outcomes for infants, toddlers, and preschoolers, especially those with special needs (Camilli et al., 2010; Epstein, 2011; Grant and Ray, 2016). These studies were built upon Epstein's original thesis of parental involvement in their children's education (Epstein, 1987; Epstein, 1995; Epstein et al., 2002).

THE EDUCATOR/PRACTITIONER ROLE
IN PARENT PARTNERSHIP

A plethora of studies shows that educating parents on effective ways to engage with educators, practitioners, and schools exist; however, the reverse is of equal importance (Epstein, 2011). Educators and practitioners must do more than simply follow procedures and prescriptions meant to help the child with a disability. They must form a network that transcends negativity and increases positive outcomes.

Epstein (2011), a seminal expert on family-school partnerships, created a comprehensive model to help parents become involved with schools and foster improved educational outcomes for their children. There are six specific keys that explain how to create partnerships that facilitate phenomenal interactions between educator/practitioner and family and how to create the partnerships (Epstein 2011; Grant and Ray, 2016).

In Epstein's (1987, 2011) framework, educators were provided with six keys that paved the way for parental engagement connections. Parenting, communicating, volunteering, learning at home, decision making, and collaborating with community were meant to assist parents' efforts to help their children when away from school settings. Training, parent programming, and additional services were part of the package that supported the well-being of the family and child (Epstein, 1987, 2011). These can easily be transferred to children found to need more specific services, as the intent is always aimed at collaboration.

One of the additional features that makes the six keys so useful is demonstrating what is possible when families, educators, practitioners, and other stakeholders collaborate for the child. As the years passed, Epstein expanded her work, and other scholars developed her ideas further, so that partnerships between educator/practitioner and family were woven together in such a way that children were the beneficiaries, and those with disabilities received the care and support needed (Epstein, 2011; Harvard Family Research Project, 2014; Mapp and Kuttner, 2013; Merrill, 2015).

Epstein's philosophy of family-school engagement was re-energized by the Harvard Family Research Project, begun in 2014. A "complimentary learning approach . . . and array of school and non-school supports complement one another to create an integrated set of community-wide resources that support learning and development from birth to young adulthood" (Harvard Family Research Project, 2014, n.p.).

Similar to Epstein's model, Mapp and Kuttner (2013) suggest a dual capacity-building framework for family-school partnerships. Endorsed by Arne Duncan, former U.S. secretary of education, the dual capacity-building framework acts as a "compass . . . to chart a path toward effective family engagement efforts that are linked to student achievement and school improvement" (p. 6), not a "blueprint for engagement initiatives" (p. 6). There are four parts to the compass that are considered essential elements: challenge, opportunity conditions, policy and program goals, and, last, family and staff capacity outcomes.

"Challenge" refers to the lack of opportunity by families, staff, and school to build partnerships. "Opportunity conditions" is a broad term linked to process and organizational conditions. "Process conditions" refers to collaboration, interactivity, and linking knowledge to learning, while "organizational conditions" are tied to systemic change, integrated change in all programs, and sustained change using resources.

Within the policy and program goals, Mapp and Kuttner (2013) refer to the four C's: capabilities (skills and knowledge), connections (networks), cognition (values and beliefs), and confidence (self-efficacy). Family and staff capacity outcomes are twofold: (1) the school and staff are tasked with connecting family engagement to student learning, creating a welcoming school culture, and honoring family knowledge; and (2) families are tasked with supporting, encouraging, advocating, and collaborating, which ultimately aid in student achievement and school culture (Mapp and Kuttner, 2013). These concepts are further examined in later chapters.

Educators and practitioners can also use community collaboration to build cooperative partnerships, increase trust between stakeholders, and work toward closing the achievement gap (National Education Association [NEA], 2013). The National Education Foundation (NEA, 2013) also provides assistance to bring together families and educators/practitioners. Although collaboration can sometimes be difficult, and the two sides may struggle to find common ground, being open and honest helps secure a promising future for the child in need (NEA, 2013).

MEETING FAMILIES WHERE THEY ARE

There are several small changes educators and practitioners can make to meet families and begin to form relationships. Equally important, there are larger, more in-depth opportunities available to practitioners and educators that ensure collaboration and interaction among families, students with disabilities, and the practitioner/educator.

Communication, Meetings, and Events

Building in daily interactions, such as communication logs, ensures that parents know how their child did during the day, especially if their child is nonverbal. A long report is not necessary, just a quick update. Likewise, parents may respond to the staff so that they know how the child's night and morning went. This can also be accomplished with online apps that translate so that families and staff can communicate regardless of the language, and, consequently, language barriers disappear.

Schedules can be tricky, and working around the family schedule is no different. For many students with exceptionalities, parents are working while the student is at school or in a care program. It is important, therefore, to offer meeting times and activities that do not interfere with work schedules. In order to accommodate families for meetings, trainings, events, and therapies, those leading the events may need to schedule early morning, late afternoon, or evening meetings.

An interesting idea, home parties are similar to Tupperware parties in that parents can invite other families to their house with the child, along with a teacher, practitioner, or other community member. The educator, practitioner, or community member offers a short presentation on a topic that is helpful to the family of the child, such as increasing vocabulary, personal care, family networking, or community services to give families respite or help (Mead, 2017).

To ensure educators and practitioners are able to partner with parents with confidence and understanding, professional development is an obvious necessity. Home visit programs offer a less formal setting for a "get to know you" session where the focus is not on academics but on learning about the family and the student.

Professional Development

Professional development for educators and practitioners surrounding ways to collaborate with families must occur at the school and district level. This type of support cannot be a "one and done" training, but rather a continued event over time. Offerings should include easy-to-employ ideas to engage families, role-playing best practices for speaking with families of students with exceptionalities, working with diverse families, and understanding cultural competencies. One area that builds and improves partnerships is connecting with families in their own surroundings. This is accomplished through a home visit program.

Home Visit Programs

Studies suggest that home visits should be general and used as a way to get to know the family, but at times they may also have a particular focus, such as possible disability, poverty, language barriers, and/or parents who lack the training to extend home learning. Home visits encourage educators to "walk in a parent's shoes" while getting to know the family better (Harvard Family Research Project, 2014; van Voorhis et al., 2013; Wight, Chau, and Aratani, 2010). While home visits are not the only way to partner with families, they are a convenient and visible way to connect, and often taking the first step makes the difference.

The home visit program helps families, who often feel alone in the disability struggle, connect with educators and practitioners. The collaboration becomes the catalyst for change as the two sides get to know each other in less formal settings, often at the home of the child and family. For some families who may be resistant to visits at home, a community park, library, or recreation center are alternatives that serve a similar purpose and place.

Dedicating time to build relationships is critically important. The more an educator or practitioner can do to understand the world of the family and their child with disabilities, the easier the job becomes; however, it is not something the educator or practitioner does in isolation. The family must be a willing partner, even if they need to be coached to understand their role.

CAPITALIZING ON FAMILY ABILITIES

The values, attitudes, and beliefs of parents regarding child development and education have a direct impact on child outcomes (Epstein, 2011; Grant and Ray, 2016; Harvard Family Research Project, 2014; Mapp and Kuttner, 2013). It is impossible to adequately address the needs of infants, toddlers, and preschoolers without considerable contributions from the family. Redefining family engagement means creating integrated community-wide programs to help children succeed. These programs can include after-school care, tutoring, parenting classes, and the like.

The expanded definition of family engagement rests on research showing how parents play significant roles in supporting their young children's growth and development, not only in the home, but also by guiding their children successfully through complex community and school systems. It is important that families become vocal advocates for their children's learning through shared responsibility and experiences (Epstein, 2011; Flamboyan Classroom Family Engagement Rubric, 2011, Mapp and Kuttner, 2013).

Shared responsibility includes communication from the educator, nurse, school counselor, or other member of the school to family members and focuses on addressing ways in which they can contribute to their child's developmental and educational success. This is not just asking for participation to occur, it is agreeing to specific roles for the educator/practitioner, school, and/or community partner, as well as the family. These roles may include having the educator check in weekly with the family or the community partner offering a service to the family.

Shared responsibility depends heavily on the situation and the idea of mutual willingness, which may inhibit contributions, thus directly impeding the success of the child (Epstein, 2011; Hynes, 2014; Mapp and Kuttner,

2013). In all situations, though, extended family is a key ingredient to the success of the child with disabilities.

THE ROLE OF EXTENDED FAMILY

While some families find it difficult to include children with disabilities in the dynamics, an extended family that fully embraces and helps the immediate family provides a much more solid base for development. Grandparents, parental siblings, cousins, and other relatives can ease the burden that many families feel when a child is diagnosed and has to receive additional support (Harris and Bruey, 2016). It is important, therefore, that they be given as much information as possible to be helpful.

Regardless of whether the disability is visible or not, engaging extended family soon and often after diagnosis is the best strategy (Vergean, 2011). Three key pieces of information are necessary for the extended family to know: (1) what help the immediate family needs; (2) what strategies will help the child; and (3) during family events, how to not focus on the disability but treat the child like other youngsters (Vergean, 2011).

Involving extended family can be as simple as having help at home or at the doctor's office, or as extensive as attending IFSP and IEP meetings. Appointments and meetings can be stressful and emotional for the family. Having an additional support person to listen and help with decision making can be invaluable. Immediate family should also share articles and videos that may be helpful to the extended family to understand the diagnosis or know how to help (Harris and Bruey, 2016).

Identifying the disability allows families to strategize and plan so that the immediate family has help and the extended family feels comfortable with the child and the situation. Other ways the extended family can support the immediate family include attending therapy sessions and volunteering at preschool or special events.

DEVELOPMENT OF FAMILY SELF-EFFICACY

For families of students with exceptionalities, it is important to be comfortable and confident in their understanding of the disability, ability to help the child, and decision-making process. This can be accomplished in a number of ways, including building confidence through adult education and using interpreters for families who desire them (Mead, 2017). Once families feel able to advocate for their child and themselves, they become more confident and ready to connect.

CONNECTING AND COLLABORATING
TO PROVIDE MANDATED SERVICES

Making connections with families and providing services may seem like a simple concept. A child is diagnosed with a disability, the family is offered and accepts support—end of story. There is much more, however, to consider for the child with a disability. Understanding what the disability is and how best to support both child and family takes a team of doctors, practitioners, and educators. Deciding where and when services will take place and who will be responsible for outcomes is an important part of the process. All of this requires communication and collaboration, a multifaceted partnership.

Early intervention services are determined by the IFSP for infants and toddlers ages birth to two years, eleven months, and may include in-home therapies or require that the family go to a specific location. Using the IFSP as a guide, it is vital that the providers and families partner to work for the benefit of the child. Often there will be an at-home or homework-type component to the services needed by the infant or toddler (U.S. Department of Health and Human Services and U.S. Department of Education, 2015).

Once the child turns three and until the child is five, he or she is entitled to attend public preschool with associated intervention and services that are determined by the IEP. High-quality preschools must also include typically developing peers at a ratio of at least one to one.

In both cases, the child who has speech or language needs may be pulled out for services, while a child with autism may spend time with nondisabled peers for part of the day and receive individualized and specific support to meet the needs identified in the IFSP or the IEP. Regardless of the disability, inclusion is considered the gold standard as a way to begin to socialize and help the child prepare for life (U.S. Department of Health and Human Services and U.S. Department of Education, 2015).

FINAL THOUGHTS

Partnering with families on behalf of children is the most basic connection educators can make, yet this vital collaboration provides the link to greater academic success for our children from birth and throughout their academic career (Grant and Ray, 2016; Mapp and Kuttner, 2013). While important for all, these parent partnerships are more significant for children with disabilities.

A successful connection between practitioners, educators, and parents is essential to the success of our youngest children (van Voorhis et al., 2013). Such a connection refers to a partnership in which parents, practitioners, and educators work together in a variety of ways to ensure the success of the student across all developmental, social, and academic settings. Unfortunately, research shows this connection is often difficult to create and maintain (Cox-Peterson, 2011; Grant and Ray, 2016).

Educators and practitioners serve as the crucial link between practice and policy, community and institution, and administrator and family (Duncan, 2015; Epstein, 2011). Educators and practitioners are assigned the difficult task of being exceptional teachers in the classroom; interventionists at home, in the school, or in the alternative environment; and skilled networkers who engage with families and the communities in which they work and live (Duncan, 2015).

Together, practitioners and educators must carefully and continually build strong relationships with families. Regardless of the setting, and specifically for children between birth and age five, the challenge is to find the most effective approaches to successfully partner with families in a way that allows everyone to address and close developmental and learning gaps together (Epstein, 2011; Grant and Ray, 2016; Mapp and Kuttner, 2013).

POINTS TO REMEMBER

- *Partnerships between families and educators/practitioners ensure developmental and educational success for our youngest populations.*
- *The first model of family engagement was created by Epstein (1987) with six keys to facilitate meaningful interactions between families and educators/practitioners. The matrix gives examples of what these interactions look like in a variety of settings, making it easy to see how this might be accomplished.*
- *The dual-capacity framework (Mapp and Kuttner, 2013) built upon Epstein's concepts to include more open-ended opportunities that would guide the work, not determine the work in advance.*
- *The Home Visit Project gives families a chance to meet with educators and practitioners in the comfort of their own home or neighborhood before going into unfamiliar surroundings, thus alleviating some of the nervousness that accompanies new opportunities.*
- *Sharing the responsibilities and burdens of a child with disabilities with the extended family creates a larger support base, gives the parents help and additional resources, and increases the potential for the child's success.*

Chapter 5

Multicultural Considerations for Young Children and Their Families

Schools are becoming increasingly diverse as families move from other countries to the United States, which necessitates that teachers become proficient in recognizing the cultural beliefs and values of their students' families (U.S. Department of Health and Human Services, 2017). The majority of teaching staff come from European American middle-class families and lack the knowledge of working with diverse families. In most schools, only 13 percent of educators represent minorities and only 6 percent of speech-language pathologists do (Kummerer, 2010). Educator-preparation programs offer little coursework in understanding diversity, which leaves staff at a loss for designing culturally responsive classrooms and teaching practices (Mead, 2017).

Educators in programs that serve children and families need to think beyond the word "diversity" as meaning "differences," but rather as the creation of an inclusive environment in all activities undertaken by a school, agency, or organization. According to Merriam-Webster (2017), diversity is "the condition of having or being composed of differing elements: variety; especially: the inclusion of different types of people (such as people of different races or cultures) in a group or organization" (n.p.).

Beyond diversity, inclusiveness must also be addressed. By definition, inclusiveness offers the family a sense of belonging and connectedness, allows for natural context and environments, encourages families to understand a wide range of abilities and the continuum of development, and includes policies and procedures that encourage all children to have equity in opportunities that support their growth and development (Bienia, 2016).

The Division of Early Childhood of the Council for Exceptional Children (Council for Exceptional Children, 2017) specifically addresses the need for programs to respect diverse family cultures, values, and linguistic backgrounds. Using the home language of the family is imperative, especially for them to understand the content of meetings and education plans. The council suggests that in order to have professional collaboration, teachers and care professionals must build partnerships based on respect for one another's cultural understandings (Council for Exceptional Children, 2017).

A policy statement issued by the U.S. Department of Health and Human Services and the U.S. Department of Education (2015) requires that all children have the opportunity to be enrolled in inclusion programs that support children from various cultures and different family backgrounds for lifelong learning. The statement advocates educator professional development that includes the staff's delving into their biases and cultural beliefs as they prepare learning environments and plan inclusive activities (U.S. Department of Education, 2015).

The policy further requires that all staff have the knowledge and the skills to work with families and that teachers use a variety of strategies to help families understand. It is important that early childhood educators become familiar with their community, attend events, and learn about the families that live within the community (Phillips, 2017). Most programs spend little time understanding the role bilingualism plays in the development of children and how it impacts their families' interaction with educators (Michael-Luna, 2015). Promoting dialogues with families and giving them opportunities to volunteer in programs fosters cultural growth (U.S. Department of Health and Human Services, 2015).

Preservice training for early childhood educators includes little subject content about working with the complexity of diverse families; however, programs that include how different family structures impact teachers' classrooms give valuable knowledge that prepare teachers to work with the diverse nuances of both the child and family (Turner-Vorbeck, 2013; SELD, 2013). Educators and practitioners who have taken time for specific coursework that evaluates their biases, attitudes, assumptions, and experiences with a diverse population of families have found that they have new perspectives on working with a diverse population and can make changes in their teaching pedagogy to more accurately reflect the families and children in front of them (Turner-Vorbeck, 2013).

A recent study found that families have the desire to share, but educators are often ill prepared to receive or act on such information (Tobin, Arzubiaga, and Adair, 2013). Teachers bring to the classroom their own culture, what they know, and what they have experienced; therefore, programs that create culturally responsive curricula recognize how family beliefs, values, parenting styles, and understanding of child development influence educators' ability to work with their students in a positive manner.

Teacher-preparation programs and ongoing professional development are needed to increase educator competencies for working with diverse families and their children in inclusive classrooms (U.S. Department of Health and Human Services and Department of Education, 2015). Programs that spend time and resources to support teachers reap the benefits of educators who are knowledgeable about working with diverse populations and who increase the success of students (Tran, 2014).

UNDERSTANDING OUR FAMILIES

Preschool teachers realize that it is imperative to know and understand the backgrounds of all the parents of the children in the class, not just from a superficial perspective but in understanding what motivates them, their cultural and familial backgrounds, and how they make decisions about their children. Many families who are faced with the realization that their child may have special needs go through a grieving process, as discussed in chapter 2. Well-prepared preschool teachers are able to support families through this process by knowing how a particular family functions and what cultural beliefs and values are instilled in the family; thus, the family will find the special education process more fulfilling and the outcomes more satisfying (Kummerer, 2010).

No matter the origins of the family, each comes to the education setting protective of their children and ready to participate in decision making at a level they are comfortable with. Families differ in their ability to be part of the decision-making process, and educators need to be aware of how to work with them. All decisions, whether program related or not, need to be made in the best interest of the child. Though institutions are thought to be school-centric, keeping the child at the center of all decision making enables the family to better understand what is appropriate and how the decision will affect their youngster (Gillanders, McKinney, and Ritchie, 2012).

Each family brings with them their own understanding of cultural norms based on what they have previously experienced and learned throughout their lifetime and through their elders. Families first need to externalize experiences that they believe their parents had before they can begin to internalize new beliefs and cultural norms in the United States (Mead, 2017). Classroom teachers can be instrumental in helping families learn new child-rearing traditions that are more appropriate than those they knew previously.

For some parents, feeding their child until they are school age is a family tradition, and teachers may be asked to continue this tradition in their classroom (Bradshaw, 2012). Explaining which tasks are developmentally and age appropriate will aid parents to internalize their role in helping their child develop self-help skills. In other cases, families may believe that "their babies" are too young to read and therefore do not expose their children to books. Changing a parental mindset is often difficult, but not for a well-trained teacher or practitioner when given the proper tools (Mead, 2017).

Creating Positive Environments

A positive environment created by practitioners, classroom teachers, and schools fosters growth in families, making connectedness to the community more beneficial. This aids in creating and understanding the goals that they have for the children. The classroom of an educator who spends time learning about the cultural norms of his or her families displays relevance that reflects the students' backgrounds. Areas in the room or close to the room where families can congregate to talk to one another build a sense of connectedness between school and home. Classroom environments should have play items, books, and curricular materials that represent the families' countries of origin (NAEYC, 2016).

Teachers should have input in the environments outside of their classroom as well. Entrance areas, hallways, and cafeteria areas with displays that mirror the families' countries of origin leads to feelings of belonging. Areas where families congregate should have items to use and play with that represent their homeland. These spaces can use books, posters, and tablecloths to make the areas more family friendly and to develop a sense of community (NAEYC, 2016)

Home Visits as a Way to Understand Families

Home visits are an effective way to learn about the family, view parental practices, help parents guide their child's learning, and understand the context of the family needs. A comprehensive study completed over a five-year period found that educators "viewed home visits as an opportunity to learn about children's backgrounds; to explain their behaviors at school; to develop comfortable relationships with parents; to reduce students' anxiety about school; and to reaffirm the varied roles that parents play in their children's learning" (Meyers, Mann, and Becker, 2011, p. 8).

Some school districts have put more formal home visit programs into practice, often detailing the number of visits per year or month, duration, content, and outcomes expected. The Parents as Teachers Program (Parents as Teachers [PAT], 2017), an evidence-based national home-visiting model, is an example of a formalized program with curriculum and other specifics to increase family competencies in working with their children. Another national program, the Parent Teacher Home Visit Program (2016), originated in California as a way to gain respect between families and their children's teachers, set goals, understand each other, and increase family-school partnerships.

For some families, the idea of a home visit may be threatening to them, as their living conditions may be different from the norm. Often, families new to schools may share a home with multiple families, live in poverty, or be afraid of identification. These factors may impact their willingness to take part in a visit. If a family is resistant to a teacher coming into their home, meeting at a local park or library may be a viable option.

When an initial visit shows that the family is becoming comfortable with the situation, then it is time to ask more questions to learn about and understand the family. The crux of the visit should be to hear about the dreams and wishes the family has for their child, what traditions are important to them, and how they celebrate holidays.

Overcoming Barriers

Families come to US schools and encounter all types of barriers. It is the goal of programs to remove as many barriers as possible, resulting in families who can fully engage with their child's school. Barriers such as language, parental education, working hours, and transportation can be readily accommodated with enough foresight on the part of the educator and school administration. A protocol should be in place that identifies families who need accommodations resulting in services that are secured quickly (Mead, 2017).

Use of Interpreters

An interpreter who has been trained in, understands, and can explain complex educational terms to the family prior to the meeting is a valuable asset in ensuring the meeting goes smoothly. Prior to the meeting, it is important to explain terms that will be used, thus helping families to feel more comfortable during the meeting, as they will have an understanding of the context of the discussion. It also lessens the chance of the family feeling overwhelmed and intimidated by the process (Han, 2012; Mead, 2017).

Interpreters who are well trained in cultural responsivity help educators and specialists recognize families' strengths and areas for improvement. Interpreters can help educators view families' protective factors as strengths and help to build bridges between parents and the school. Cultural protective factors are practices that support families and include cultural beliefs regarding the importance of the family, such as *familismo*, religious affiliation, and *simpatia* (Knoche, Marvin, and Sheridan, 2014; FitzGerald, 2011). Familismo is important to the Hispanic culture and illustrates itself in many ways, such as the activities that families participate in or the educational attitudes and beliefs that are common among its population (FitzGerald, 2011; Jasis and Ordonez-Jasis, 2012).

Protective factors help families to be flexible in understanding and receiving services, as well as in developing positive partnerships (Knoche et al., 2014). An interpreter who knows the different cultural factors one operates under can help build bridges between teachers and their students' parents, which in essence empowers families and fosters trusting relationships (Knoche et al., 2014).

Understanding Systems

Though special education laws mandate what must be offered to families and how students' schooling is to be shaped, educational systems vary between countries and between states (IDEA, n.d.). Families who come to the United States with children who have identified disabilities may have experienced services in their native country and expect the same in the United States. Due to the variances among countries, what a family may have previously deemed appropriate may not be what is offered to the child in the new educational setting (Heer, Rose, and Larkin, 2016).

Many parents may have a limited understanding of the educational systems in the United States, resulting in differing expectations for services, which may undermine the confidence levels of families (Han, 2012; U.S. Department of Education and U.S. Department of Health and Human Services, 2017). Having resources available for families to reach out to before the parent meeting will help them identify similarities and differences, and assimilate to the systems they are now operating under (Han, 2012).

Each state has a special education resource center that has bilingual educators who can assist parents in understanding what is forthcoming for services for their child. Local advocacy groups can be sought by calling the state's resource center (U.S. Department of Education and U.S. Department of Health and Human Services, 2017).

Cultural Responsiveness

Sylvia, a home visitor, was invited into the home of one of her new students, Pedro. He was three years old and ready to begin part-time in her class. The visit was informal, as Sylvia wanted to find out about the family, their dreams for Pedro, and the interests he had. This would allow Sylvia to tailor her instruction to his needs and likes. Pedro's parents shared his likes and dislikes, what their dreams for him were, and some of the struggles Pedro had. Pedro used little self-initiated language, for example, asking for a toy, or saying "Hi" and "Bye."

Pedro's parents went on to tell Sylvia that he didn't sleep in his bed or have a nightly routine. Sylvia listened quietly and then offered several suggestions about how Pedro might begin sleeping in his own bed, how to establish routines, and what his parents should do to get him ready for school. Sylvia went on to explain that they should put a favorite toy out of reach until Pedro uses language to ask for it. Sylvia was pleased with the visit and looked forward to the next one. When she called to schedule it, the parents told her they weren't interested in another home visit.

After several attempts to schedule another visit, Sylvia spoke to her colleagues, who commented that she treaded on cultural dispositions that the family probably felt were none of her business. Historically, co-sleeping is a practice used by many Hispanic families (Bradshaw, 2012). Often, Pedro would fall asleep in his parents' bed when he was ready. Since both parents worked long hours, the idea of a regimented evening routine was beyond their expectations.

In many cultures, children are taught not to interrupt siblings and adults. Even at an early age, children learn these cultural patterns (Durand, 2011). In this case, this most likely influenced the strategies that the family was comfortable in using. Sylvia had touched on cultural practices that were sacred with the family. Parental ethno-theories are deep-seated beliefs that families follow in the raising of their children (Froesen, Hanson, and Martin, 2015). Instead, Sylvia should have mostly listened during the home visit in order to gain understanding of the family. Instead, she offered too much of her own perceptions on the right way to parent.

Developing a culturally responsive classroom and attitude is vital to understanding the families whose students are provided services (Michael-Luna, 2015). As a service provider, positive interactions that are reflective of families' beliefs and values must be the norm (Bradshaw, 2012; Heer et al., 2016). In Sylvia's case, she crossed that line, assuming her beliefs were the correct ones, and offered advice devoid of cultural responsiveness. Educators who examine and reflect on their own culture have a better understanding of how it intersects with families' beliefs and values (Durand, 2011).

What teachers consider normal may not be what is expected from a family. Understanding how to interface with families who have different ideas about "normal" is premier to being a successful special education teacher (Durand, 2011). Bradshaw (2012) proposes a framework for providing culturally responsive services. Four pillars must be in place: examining one's own culture; acquiring knowledge of client cultures; building culturally competent practices; and reflecting and evaluation practices.

When the first two pillars are well understood, culturally responsive practices can be put in place. Reflecting on strategies that have worked, sharing with others, and refining teaching practices strengthen service providers' ability to be effective with families in the program (Bradshaw, 2012; Rogers-Sirin, Ryce, and Sirin, 2014).

TEACHER PERCEPTIONS OF FAMILIES

Along with developing a culturally responsive classroom, teachers' own perceptions about families need to be kept in check (Phillips, 2017). Assumptions about why a parent chooses or does not choose to do certain things is not for educators to comment on (Raty, 2010). Assuming that parents "don't care" because they don't attend family nights may be incorrect (Johnson, 2015). Other factors may contribute to the lack of engagement, such as parents' own experiences in school, unintentional intimidation by teachers, and a lack of both process and organizational conditions to engage parents (Mapp, 2014). Other pundits (Gillanders et al., 2012) would argue that schools are school-centric, and activities involving parent engagement are based on the institutional missions and aimed at the white middle-class population.

Teachers who understand the dynamics of the household and realize that both parents work two jobs quickly acknowledge the confines the household operates within and make other arrangements to accommodate the family for conferences and other student-based issues (Han, 2011). Families who have children with special needs may need more understanding than those without special needs children (Heer et al., 2016). Instead of making assumptions regarding how the family functions, an educated teacher can be more tactful in how he or she works with its members, thus changing his or her perceptions (Han, 2011).

Teacher Transfer of Knowledge

Educators and practitioners are proficient at explaining to families the why's and how's of the early childhood classroom, how special education techniques and strategies work, and how parents can parent. Unfortunately, while wearing a teacher's hat, many educators forget about other skills they possess. As a parent, an educator may have great parenting skills and strategies that can be shared; however, while wearing the teacher's hat, knowledge transfer doesn't take place.

Originally used as an organizational theory, knowledge transfer is valuable to teaching. Defined as transferring knowledge from one employee to another, the term is valuable in the education profession in two ways

(Cancialosi, 2014). One is the transfer of knowledge from one educator to another educator. This may be during a coaching model, when one proficient teacher explains strategies to another. The second form of transfer is from an educator to a parent; however, while wearing the educator's hat, disruptive knowledge transfer takes place. The educator is not able to move out of his or her role of teacher to talk about what the educator is also proficient in outside the education field.

An educator, for example, can explain the need for family-school partnerships but, when trying to deal with difficult parental concerns about their child, may not be able to remove the educator's hat to empathize with the family's concern. Practicing these skills will make the job of switching between "educator" and "parent teacher" easier.

Unconscious Intimidation

Teachers, through no fault of their own, may appear to intimidate families during interactions with them and when explaining educational terms or practices. Additionally, based on past experiences, parents may have their own assumptions and perceptions that further the feelings of intimidation (Raty, 2010). Due to these experiences, parents may become fearful or intimidated by educators (Raty, 2010). Teachers who sit at a round table during conferences or next to the child while speaking with parents have better results in communicating with parents and may choose not to use educational terms or those not frequently used in the parents' vocabulary (Mead, 2017).

Educators who ask many questions to check for understanding while talking with parents will find this technique valuable (Mead, 2017). Staff who emphasize that they speak *with* parents, not *at* them, while using reflectivity and "I" questions to check for understanding, are most successful (Mead, 2017). Waiting three to five seconds after asking a question is best, as parents may be processing and translating their response (Cheathum and Ostrosky, 2009).

Connectedness and Safety

Families need to have a feeling of connectedness to their schools (Mead, 2017). Connectedness goes beyond a feeling of belonging. Anyone can feel they belong to a school since their child attends it. Belonging is feeling connected in a variety of ways: with teachers, the principal, lunch staff, the bus driver, and other school staff. Having positive, meaningful two-way conversations that revolve around the needs of the child offers the parents the ability to improve their communication skills in a relaxed way (Mapp, 2014). These conversations lead to families who feel that their children are safe and well cared for at school (Mead, 2017).

Leadership for Developing Inclusive Classrooms and Engaging Parents

The IDEA law mandates that students with special needs spend the majority of their day in classrooms with typical peers or less restrictive environments, unless the child's education plan specifies the need for self-contained classrooms (IDEA, n.d.). With more students mainstreamed, coupled with teachers who have been mandated to take coursework in working with children with special needs, schools are on the edge of positive changes to reflect their student population (Phillips, 2017). At the same time, school leadership is implementing models that foster both cultural and family growth, and are better defining how to engage all parents in their child's schooling (Mapp, 2014; Phillips, 2017).

Understanding Engagement as an Evolving Process

In 2011, Ferlazzo redefined the concept of parent "involvement" to become family "engagement." In doing so, he used simple dictionary definitions: "involve is to 'enfold or envelope,' whereas one of the meanings of engage is 'to come together and interlock.' Thus involvement implies *doing to*; in contrast, engagement implies *doing with*" (Ferlazzo, 2011, p. 10). Additionally, Mapp (2014) began the use of "family" instead of parent, as it reflects the diversity of a household, to include biological parents, grandparents, aunts, and uncles, as well as foster parents and others charged with the care of children (Mead, 2017).

The transformation of terminology enabled the field of education to develop methods to engage parents in the development of the actual process and in providing school districts with a systemic progression in their school-family partnership (Mapp and Kuttner, 2013). Developing a relationship-building process ensures that positive school-family engagement systems will be achieved (Mapp and Kuttner, 2013).

To further the systemic processes around school-family communities, the U.S. Department of Education's Family and Community Engagement Division contracted with Karen Mapp to develop a family and school engagement framework that could be used universally (K. Mapp, personal communication, April 8, 2014). In April 2014, the federal department released "Dual Capacity-Building Framework for Family-School Partnerships" (Mapp, 2014). This document provides educational institutions with a framework of process and organizational conditions, policy and program goals, and family and staff outcomes to support active partnerships (Duncan, 2014; Mapp, 2014).

Additionally, this hallmark framework provides schools with a solid foundation to embellish their family-school partnerships while the demographics of their populations show more inclusiveness of households from all over the world and for children with varied needs (Duncan, 2014). Schools that implement this framework are able to reap the benefits of having a successful school-family partnership system that increases engagement and student achievement, especially for those who have emigrated from other countries (Mapp, 2014).

Mapp (2014) defines process conditions from the dual-capacity building framework as a "series of actions, operations, and procedures that are part of any activity or initiative" (p. 10). Process conditions must be "linked to learning; relational; developmental; collective and interactive" (Mapp, 2014, p. 1). Organizational processes are those conditions in place that help initiatives to be implemented and sustained. The organizational conditions included in the framework are those that are systemic, integrated, and sustained (Mapp, 2014).

Hispanic families' historical perspective, for example, maintains they should attend school events and activities only when invited and that there is a true separation between school and home; thus, until these conditions, such as personal invitations and positive phone calls, are put into place and fully understood by all parties, the mismatching of family engagement ideals will continue to be in conflict (Gillanders et al., 2012).

FINAL THOUGHTS

Educators, institutional leadership, practitioners, and others who support children and their families need to recognize the importance of programs that are culturally responsive to developing home-school partnerships. Knowing the laws that schools must abide by is only half the equation to success. Each family has their own cultural terms about their homes and children that relate directly to what they do. Educators who fully understand the meanings of these terms have an appreciation of the family's culture, and it shows in their interactions.

Institutions that support leadership development of educators and staff and that intentionally provide training on being culturally responsive find that there is increased communication between families and schools, and the implementation is then more meaningful. Educators who have the knowledge, tools, and attitudes to understand and welcome families are motivated to provide inclusive classrooms.

All those who help families to understand the special education process, break down barriers, and recognize the strengths they bring to education develop better relationships. When families realize that educators understand and appreciate their culture, the diversity that was originally thought of as a barrier will be seen as an asset for the developing child with special needs.

POINTS TO REMEMBER

- *Culture is an asset to all programs; inclusive schools and programs can be built around the families who will use them.*
- *Cultural barriers can be overcome by asking questions to seek understanding. Home visits are an excellent way to learn about the family.*
- *The classroom environment should reflect the cultures of the children in the room.*
- *Accommodations are required under the law and, in most cases, are easy to obtain. Increased communication with families will develop an understanding of what is appropriate in a least restrictive environment.*
- *Families and their children from other countries deserve to be educated in a safe environment and be given opportunities to understand U.S. educational systems.*
- *Educators need to be knowledgeable about their students' cultural backgrounds in order to understand how their assumptions and biases affect their teaching abilities.*
- *Being proactive requires that leadership be the catalyst of school reform leading to cultural responsiveness and inclusive classrooms.*

Chapter 6

Supporting Cognitive Development to Benefit Learning

Cognition is the ability to think using well-developed processes within the brain to interpret sensory input and to guide social and motor actions (Bjorklund and Causey, 2018; Berk, 2017; *Psychology Today*, 2017). It is also defined as "processes of the mind that lead to 'knowing'" (Berk, 2017, p. 225). Berk (2017) acknowledges that cognition "includes mental activity of attending, remembering, symbolizing, categorizing, planning, reasoning, problem solving, creating and fantasizing" (p. 225). Cognition development is not static, but rather changes over time, dependent on the type of environment to which a child is exposed.

FACTORS THAT INFLUENCES COGNITION

There are multiple factors that influence the development of cognition. Families that have a lower socioeconomic status often offer less stimulation to their children, due to the fact that they do not know how to encourage the development of cognition, while families with higher income create more desirable learning environments (Bann et al., 2015).

Early intervention for children identified with learning needs is critical to closing the achievement gap of those who live in low-income homes, who lack stimulation, or who live in families that lack the skills to be role models (Bjorklund and Causey, 2018). Other factors that influence cognitive development include biological or genetic factors, whether babies are preterm, and low birth weight, as well as the social environment the child lives in (Bjorklund and Causey, 2018).

Additional factors that influence development are the intensity of reactions as well as the levels and duration of interactions from adults that create either a positive or negative environment. This leads to the age-old question of *nature versus nurture* and how biology or nurturing promotes or hinders development. Every educator has his or her own opinion on this question, depending on their life experiences, how they were raised, and perhaps, how they have chosen to raise their own children, if applicable.

A world devoid of social stimulation and activities with others, in most cases, results in children who have large gaps in opportunities to learn; conversely, homes with highly educated parents, who talk with their children and have multiple interactions with them, have less of a gap (Bann et al., 2015). Children with high-risk factors may be qualitatively different in how they think and process information (Bjorklund and Causey, 2018). Though it is difficult to quantify how children think, educators usually measure it through observation (Berk, 2017; Bjorklund and Causey, 2018).

Jean Piaget, a developmental theorist, posits that adults who offer stimulating learning environments can observe children as they go through the continuum of development (Miller, 2016). Piaget's four stages of development have been a key theory in the development of children (Henniger, 2013). Schemas or mental concepts are formed early on, and new information is then assimilated or accommodated. The four stages are: sensorimotor, preoperational, concrete operational, and formal operations (Miller, 2016). Each stage builds on the one prior as children go from being very concrete to more abstract learners (Berk, 2017; Henniger, 2013).

Sensorimotor Stage

From the minute a child is born, he/she begins to take in information from the surrounding environment. At the child's first uttering, parents show delight with cries to be fed. The infant quickly learns that crying brings food or an adult to make it more comfortable (Connecticut Early Learning and Development Standards [CT ELDS], 2014). All of these interactions are the beginning of developing relationships. Information input has a similar effect: sounds, smells, and taste become familiar to infants. Infants can recognize the scent of their mother's breastmilk in as early as three or four days, as smell is the strongest sense (Berk, 2017).

Babies soon begin to recognize voices and will turn their heads to a familiar sound, and as infants' vision becomes clearer, they begin to recognize the faces they see on a daily basis (CT ELDS, 2014). Infants around two or three months old find their hands and begin to suck or chew on them.

During this stage of development, termed by Piaget (1936) as the *sensorimotor stage*, infants through two years of life begin to mouth everything, are aware that they can make sounds and "raspberries" with their tongue, and become attached to certain items that have the scent of their main caregivers.

Once introduced to the high chair, infants of six to eight months learn cause and effect when they drop or push items off the tray and excitedly wait to see who picks it up (Berk, 2017). This is just the beginning of many development milestones.

Environments that help create nurturing trust enable mobile infants and toddlers to explore the space they are in with an adult who will respond quickly to their needs. This age group recognizes that there are main caregivers who react to them by responding to them, laughing with them, or protecting them from danger (Miller, 2016). Though children at this stage will try to outdo their caregivers and parents by testing limits, their cognitive growth depends on the responsiveness of caring adults (Gestwicki, 2017). Adults who actively respond to children begin to make concrete connections—making new assumptions or taking in new ideas to assimilate to what they already know (Berk, 2017).

Preoperational Stage

As infants move into toddlerhood, they love motion, banging into things, mouthing toys, trying new foods, looking at books, asking questions, testing limits, and exploring their environments (Gestwicki, 2017). Toward the end of age two, children move into the *preoperational stage*, which can go through seven years of age (Miller, 2016). This stage is dominated by massive growth in their language, word usage, and question asking. During this stage, it is not words that drive cognition, but rather "sensorimotor activity leads to internal images of experience, which children then label with words" (Berk, 2017, p. 239).

The preoperational stage brings about more play by engaging other children, and sociodramatic play becomes less self-centered and uses more complex themes (Miller, 2016). During this stage, children learn to attend longer to activities either in play environments or tabletop learning, that is, tabletop blocks, sorting, and classifying. Children show eagerness to learn by seeking out new learning experiences and are willing, at most times, to bring a task to completion (CT ELDS, 2014).

The cause and effect that was seen during the middle-infant stage takes on a new meaning. Science experiments, setting up rail tracks and running cars up and down them, and being able to make a hypothesis of what will happen are notable during this stage (Gestwicki, 2017). Preschoolers begin to differentiate between their likes and dislikes: they can sort by multiple attributes and see simple ABA and ABBA patterns.

New social-emotional development includes an awareness of others and developing empathy that leads children to take on more complex cognitively challenging learning (Berk, 2017; Gestwicki, 2017). Those who work with young children begin to see signs that they are becoming less self-centric and start to understand other perspectives. This allows children to solve more complex problems, use multiple strategies to solve problems, and use previous knowledge to build new concepts. At this time, young children become quite proud of their accomplishments and look for approval from other children (CT ELDS, 2014).

GROWTH PROGRESSIONS AND LEARNING STYLES

Children are on a growth trajectory that, if well supported, allows them to acquire skills necessary for school and beyond (Miller, 2016). This path is founded on a theory of child development: children learn skills when they have enough foundational knowledge to acquire, assimilate, and accommodate new information (Berk, 2017; Gestwicki, 2017). Unfortunately, there are times when programs and parents push children beyond what they are capable of doing.

To help illustrate this point, it is important to understand that the brain takes in new information, processes it, and assimilates ideas, concepts, and new ways of thinking. When new information is forced upon the brain with no links to previous knowledge, it doesn't fit; thus, there is no way to support or assimilate the material. The brain is then stuck attempting to learn concepts it is not ready to integrate. Instead, repetition and deeper learning using background knowledge would be more beneficial.

Though this illustration is significant for working with typical and atypical children, Vygotsky's zone of proximal development suggests that with a good role model who has a higher level of skills, a child can learn greater cognitive, social, and physical skills (Miller, 2016). Children all have different learning styles, and a responsive educator understands how to assist each student in his or her growth (Miller, 2016).

HELPING FAMILIES UNDERSTAND
CONTINUOUS GROWTH PROGRESSION

At some point during the first four years of a school-based program, educators will be asked by parents about the tangible learning that their children are experiencing. Families of typical or atypical children look for quantitative changes (shown by testing) or product outcomes of growth (Berk, 2017). An educator who intentionally explains the validity of seeing qualitative changes, and how cognition is improved by learning "through the process" rather than the product itself, helps parents understand the growth progression. It is a vital part of working with parents to teach this valuable concept (Gestwicki, 2017).

Though there are growth scales, screening, and other tests to document a child's progress, growth is not a race to a predetermined place. Children and adults are never completely finished learning; it is an educator's responsibility to help parents to understand that learning is a progression that happens over a lifetime (CT ELDS, 2014). Many states have recently initiated or are in the process of revising early childhood learning or developmental standards that are employing a variable growth progression or continuum, rather than cut-off scaled growth charts (CT ELDS, 2014). Educators can check with their office of early childhood or state department of education for a particular state's document.

Child-focused programs that have experiential, hands-on activities encourage children to learn by taking risks. Preschool children need to learn to be able to take risks during learning and play and not be afraid to do so (Berk, 2017). Consequently, going down the slide the wrong way, playing on a rope swing, or traversing the monkey bars are all risk-taking activities that build character. The rest of education and life is full of taking risks. Learning these critical skills during the preschool years reinforces and promotes learning that will be beneficial throughout children's lives (Berk, 2017).

The best classrooms are not led by teachers, but rather by the experiences children take part in, and educators must question whose needs should be met: an agency's or higher authority's expectations, or the needs of each individual child (Berk, 2017). These concepts may seem to be second nature to educators; however, parents who hear about the importance of preschool and early education may not understand growth progression and how developmentally appropriate programs support them (CT ELDS, 2014).

Educators who take the time, before enrollment, at open house nights, and throughout the year, to explain the components of a developmentally appropriate classroom and its relationship to growth progressions will find their job much easier and that families will become advocates for their program (Gestwicki, 2017).

SUPPORTING THE DEVELOPMENT
OF EXECUTIVE FUNCTION

Executive functioning (EF) is a child's ability to use "higher-order cognitive abilities for planning, information process and problem solving for goal-directed behaviors in novel or challenging settings" (Verdine, Irwin, Golinkoff, and Hirsh-Pasek, 2014, p. 37). Educators can plan activities that promote the components of executive function: choosing and planning, task persistence, cognitive flexibility, working memory and regulation of attention, and impulses/self-control (CT ELDS, 2014).

Berk (2017) posits that executive functioning is the "overall supervisor of the cognitive system, managing its activities to ensure we attain our goals" (p. 281). Executive function ability changes over time as the child develops. The Center on the Developing Child at Harvard University (President and Fellows at Harvard College, 2017) has a five-minute video that shows the development of executive function in children.

Infants begin to develop the first signs of executive function during the second part of the first year (Berk, 2017). Cause and effect, for example, as well as the ability to repeat an activity such as peek-a-boo, show that the infant must recall what has happened and how to repeat it to get the same effect or elicit a new one. Later in toddlerhood, watching another child set a table and trying to repeat it shows that the child is beginning to use his or her working memory and the planning parts of EF. Children in preschool show an even higher level of skills, as most behaviors are goal driven and more complex (Berk, 2017).

Children with disabilities may develop cognitive and executive skills in a different progression that then requires more support than typical children. Having a higher level of established routines that are flexible in timing but maintain the same sequence is extremely important for atypical children (Gestwicki, 2017).

Repeating a sequence of routines may seem negotiable with some children, while others require multiple reinforcements to learn the necessary patterns (Gestwicki, 2017). Children who struggle to complete a job may lack the ability to apply task persistence to see it through to completion (Center for Parenting Education, 2017). Breaking down complex tasks into smaller steps is a technique that is valuable in helping an atypical child to be successful (Gestwicki, 2017).

Visual management systems, including large vertical or horizontal schedules and computer-generated or picture boards, are techniques that support children and are intentional strategies provided for all children. As educators strive to make classrooms student centered, strategies that are used to help children become self-reliant versus expecting constant support from an adult will aid children in developing vital skills necessary to build more complex task abilities (Gestwicki, 2017).

In classrooms, educators can reinforce simple tasks, such as snack progressions: wash your hands, take a napkin, take a snack, eat, clean up, throw garbage out, and wash your hands. Atypical children may need this sequence broken down into more manageable steps, to include: take a seat, finish your snack, and so on. This is where the visual picture board comes in handy (Berk, 2017). A strategy to check if a child is grasping the sequence is to have the child use his or her picture exchange system (PECS), with the pictures not in sequence (Brody and Frost, n.d.). The child is expected to take the pictures and put them in the correct sequence, to eat the snack, and clean up.

Some children may need to start with ten to thirteen steps arranged by the teacher, and as those steps are learned, children can handle arranging their own steps with fewer pictures, resulting in eliminating steps until the children can do the task without a visual support. For other children with varied learning disabilities, the actual picture may need to be explained and shown to the child before it can be added to a picture board (Gestwicki, 2017).

Educators can help parents model the same behaviors by using a PECS system at home (Brody and Frost, n.d.). It may be necessary to include the sequence of getting dressed, toilet training, and packing a lunch or school bag to increase executive function. Some children with extreme learning needs may require a visual for all activities, whereas other children may miss steps in a sequence that needs reinforcement.

ADAPTIVE MEDIUMS AND ELECTRONICS TO SUPPORT COGNITIVE DEVELOPMENT

There are many new electronic learning toys made specifically to reinforce activities that educators expect children to accomplish. Some children are not motivated or interested to learn; however, having tangible rewards provided through low-level technology often motivates the child. Using switches to make toys automatic reinforces the accomplishment of a child (Tarrant, 2017). Toys such as a fire engine with a ladder that rises up when a child completes a task, vibrating bugs, a puppy, or music boxes are useful, depending on what motivates a child. Having switches, adapters, and jelly bean twist switches that turn battery-operated toys into reinforcing ones increases performance, which is imperative for children who learn differently (Tarrant, 2017).

Using interactive whiteboards that allow the projection of an image from a laptop or a computer, and interaction with the board through touch or specialized pens to aid learning through movement, is effective for children who need a large space to learn, have vision problems, are in wheelchairs, or experience issues with sitting (Krakower and Plante, 2016; Tarrant, 2017). Realizing the benefits of sensory input to assimilate the information into their body, Promethean boards using numerous programs have shown great promise. The boards are ideal for interactive games and for learning through music, songs, poetry, and fingerplays.

Desk work often proves difficult for children with disabilities due to their inability or discomfort in attending classes. The use of slant boards, light boards, and other interactive equipment may help children be successful. Other children respond well to pressure devices such as a weighted vest or lap blankets (Tarrant, 2017). Both devices provide feedback through their proprioceptive system, comforting children and aiding them in feeling comfortable in their chair.

Chair stability is critical to children being able to focus on their work. An adult often feels unstable when sitting on a tall stool with no foot rung or arm rail. A child who cannot place his or her feet flat on the floor experiences the same instability and quickly loses balance; conversely, a child who is well positioned, feet flat on the floor, knees and arms at a ninety-degree angle, arms on a chair rail for side-to-side stability (Community Products, LLC, 2017) and with the correct table height, can concentrate on his or her work.

Some children may need to have a sensory device within reach in order to concentrate. A sensory blanket or weighted wrap draped over children's shoulders or lap can give them something to feel while they work (Tarrant, 2017). Educators have to be conscious of the child's awareness of how other children react to such devices and be empathetic while helping other children understand that everyone learns differently, and such a device helps.

Children who concentrate closely on their work may grind their teeth or make noises with their mouth as they work. Grinding the teeth at a young age may impair the child's ability to bite and chew food; therefore, it is important that the child's pediatrician or dentist be consulted. Small chewy toys or clear fish-tank tubing on a string makes for an inexpensive mouthing device to stop grinding. Young children may need to be reminded to use it consistently if they are unaware they are grinding their teeth. There are other commercial toys and mouth devices that provide the sensory input needed to halt poor habits. Occupational therapists may be able to assist with these types of issues (Tarrant, 2017).

All children learn by doing and, when repeating concepts, use multiple and different mediums to promote memory learning, reinforce muscle memory and, if needed, build new plasticity in the brain. Textured letters and numbers, sand, or cornmeal in a box top, or shaving cream are useful for a child to draw out figures. Educators may have to use hand-over-hand facilitation to promote this type of activity for a child who has sensitivities to using such materials. For children who are resistant to putting their hands in such mediums, using brightly colored paint in a small, durable, sealable plastic bag may increase their interest to play with it.

Modern technology has increased the number of augmentative communication devices available to support children without verbal communication skills (Krakower and Plante, 2016). For older students who are already fairly proficient in their writing and texting skills, a program called Proloquo4Text is available for purchase through iTunes for iPhones, iPads, and Apple watches (Krakower and Plante, 2016). These programs can be used in multiple languages and have the capacity of teaching high-use, recorded familiar phrases, and students are able to choose their own voice (Krakower and Plante, 2016). DynaVoxes are highly effective for younger children who can identify a picture of their needs and press the button to hear a prerecording of the item (Krakower and Plante, 2016).

Educators should be familiar with other technology that is available to be used in the classroom. Not all technology needs to be high tech, expensive, or meant for children with learning needs. Other low-tech, inexpensive methods include the use of sentence boards and sequencing boards that can show a child the steps to use when needing to toilet. The number of pictures can be increased or decreased as needed. The Boardmaker program, usually found in most programs, has numerous applications: PECS (Brody and Frost, n.d.), sequence boards, setting directions for self-regulation, and augmentative communication.

TECHNOLOGY IN THE EARLY CHILDHOOD SETTING

Technology can contribute to an effectively operating early childhood setting as a part of its overall educational practice. It is important to note that teachers, students, and the US educational system all play a role in how effective technology-enhanced instruction can be for all students, specifically those who are zero to five years of age.

There is still much to learn about the science of how early childhood students relate to new media (Blackwell and Lauricella, 2013). Research over the past decade provides some insight into how young children, and at what specific ages, may develop cognitive skills from using different types of new technology. One study conducted through Northwestern University (2014) used path-modeling to investigate the relationship between extrinsic and intrinsic factors that influence early childhood educators' digital technology use.

The data from this survey of 1,234 early childhood educators nationwide reported that three factors contribute to the overall effectiveness of technology use with young children: teacher attitudes, accessibility to equipment, and student demographics (Northwestern University, 2014). Teacher attitudes toward the value of technology to aid in children's learning had the highest effect on appropriate technology use. Although educators have increased access to technology, there are still many reasons for its underuse, including the many barriers teachers encounter when attempting to integrate technology into their classrooms (Northwestern University, 2014).

Applying the unified theory of acceptance and use of technology (UTAUT) to early childhood education (Blackwell and Lauricella, 2013), one current study examined how early childhood educators use traditional and new technologies. Findings from the study of 1,329 teachers of children age birth to four showed that even though extrinsic barriers influenced access to a variety of technologies, positive beliefs in children's learning from using technology predicted its actual use (Blackwell and Lauricella, 2013).

The study also concluded that more experienced teachers had negative attitudes toward technology that exceeded those of less experienced teachers (Blackwell and Lauricella, 2013). Student socioeconomic status had the strongest effect on teacher attitudes, while support and technology policy influenced teacher confidence and therefore their aptitude (Blackwell and Lauricella, 2013).

According to a 2013 national survey of 1,200 American families, more than eight in ten children ages two to ten use digital media every week, and two-thirds have tablets or e-readers (Blackwell and Lauricella, 2013). It is vital, then, that early childhood settings provide equitable access to technology as we continue to educate the millennial child.

Prior to the technological boom in education, developmental scientists like DeLoache (Association for Psychological Science, n.d.) have long since studied "symbolic understanding" and "pictorial competence." Allen and Kelly (2015) cite these skills of infants, toddlers, and preschoolers as developmental milestones that allow them to construct meaning from what they see represented in media of all kinds.

With the focus on technology in early childhood classrooms across the United States, nearly all fifty states have adopted or used part of the International Society for Technology in Education (ISTE) student standards (Council for Accreditation of Educator Preparation [CAEP], 2013). CAEP also lists standards for teachers. CAEP (2013) asks that educators in teacher-preparatory programs learn to "use technology to enhance their teaching" and encourages them to "use technology effectively in their job role to support student learning" (p. 281).

Technology use varies widely across educational settings, as well as opinions about how good teaching should look when integrated with technology. Expectations for the use of technology in prekindergarten and childcare settings vary greatly from those in the regular elementary education system. Unfortunately, there is no widely adopted set of standards for using technology with our youngest students. As of this writing, some states do not even mention technology in their early education learning guidelines (Daugherty, Dossani, John, and Wright, 2014).

The American Academy of Pediatrics (2011) advocates that, although some preschools proudly advertise the availability of computers and smartboards, other early childhood settings take pride in having policies that keep children away from screen media of any kind. Certain states and childcare providers follow strict guidelines within the Quality Rating and Improvement System as well as various licensing systems (NCECQA, n.d.).

In an attempt to provide guidance to teachers in early childhood educational settings from birth through age eight, with regard to the effectiveness of technology in the classroom, NAEYC (2012) released a statement saying that the effectiveness of technology in early childhood was dependent on many factors, including appropriate use, developmental abilities of students, and context. It is clear that stakeholder agreement is lacking concerning how technology should be integrated into early childhood programs.

FINAL THOUGHTS

There are numerous factors that influence the development of a child's cognitive abilities. Social capital, high risks, lack of good prenatal care, and lack of a stimulating environment all play a part. Cognition is influenced by a child's home environment, caregivers and parents, educators, and learning environments. It is the basis for all future learning and can be impacted positively by educators who understand the nuances of appropriate programming and who can share its benefits with parents.

Piaget's sensory-motor phase is developed first in infancy and lasts until a child is close to six years old, although the pre-operational stage overlaps. During this time, relationships with key caregivers and parents are important to children's learning and being able to develop both their motor and cognitive skills. Both Piaget and Vygotsky believe that social-emotional development is linked to cognitive growth. Whether educators are believers of Piaget's stages of growth or Vygotsky's zone of proximal development, both theorists provide effective platforms for educators who design programs for developing children.

Educators who understand growth progressions, as well as Piaget and Vygotsky's theories, are well seated to inform parents on the concept of developmentally appropriate practice and how it reinforces curriculum and promotes learning environments. Children touching, hearing, seeing, and tasting what they are learning about solidifies cognitive development.

Executive functioning is the ability to use higher order thinking skills to plan activities, execute them, and function in daily life and across all domains of learning (President and Fellows at Harvard College, 2017). Executive functioning promotes lifelong learning, and although children who learn differently will also learn the associated skills, it may take longer, and other strategies will be important to teach.

There are many adaptive and technology-based programs that can advance children's learning. Some are low tech while others are high-tech. From simple picture boards and the use of Baggies, to speech boxes or the use of a smartphone or tablet for augmentative communication, educators have a plethora of materials to support learning.

POINTS TO REMEMBER

- *All children learn in various ways following their own growth progression, and using a variety of tools will help each child move toward his or her personal potential.*
- *Many factors influence development; educators need to be aware of them and how to navigate through the developmental stages to encourage learning.*
- *Piaget and Vygotsky have differing but equally compelling theories to assist in developing curriculum to support teaching pedagogy.*
- *Educators take on prime roles in helping to educate parents and caregivers on developmentally appropriate practice and learning strategies.*
- *Executive functioning is a lifelong skill that needs to be learned during the early years and can be supported by educators and parents.*
- *Educators who use numerous different strategies will be able to support all children, no matter what their learning style.*

Chapter 7

Physical Development

Milestones that Matter

President John F. Kennedy once said that physical fitness is important and necessary to ensure a healthy body, but also that "it is the basis of dynamic and creative intellectual activity" (Kennedy, n.d., n.p.), which begins when a child is born, and early physical development is the foundation for all other skills to be developed. Physical development includes fine, gross, and oral motor skills and impacts a child's ability to become social and intelligent (Berk, 2017). Piaget states that "sensory and motor experiences are the basis for all intellectual functioning" (Henniger, 2013, p. 333) while Montessori stresses the link between mental and physical capacity that formed the basis for her method of education (Berk, 2017).

Physical development is the fastest period of growth in all the domains, especially for youngsters under three years of age. Children under two years of age develop motor skills in spurts, and large muscles develop before fine motor muscles. Development occurs from head to toe (*cephalocaudal development*), and fine motor development occurs from the center of the body outward (*proximodistal development*) (Henniger, 2013). Berk (2017) states that the head forms first prenatally from the embryonic disk, followed by the rest of the body, from the trunk to the hands, to the fingers and legs, and to the feet and toes.

The dynamic system theory of motor development concentrates on how more complex skills are formed from primitive growth by encouraging stimulus to the central nervous system (Berk, 2017). The stimulus needed for an infant to nurse, pick up toys, lift his or her head, or roll back and forth is enough to motivate the central nervous system to develop better neurons.

It becomes the role of educators to continue this growth, provide enriching environments, adapt strategies for those who need more motivation, and break down the motivators, if necessary, to help children understand the steps

(Gestwicki, 2017). For some children with delays, the educator's role is crucial, as the child needs modeling or task breakdowns in order to be successful.

CRITICAL VERSUS SENSITIVE PERIODS OF GROWTH

Developmental psychologists have always considered two significant periods in child development: the critical period, when children have short predetermined times when they can learn skills, and the sensitive period, when the time frame for learning is broader and more open to cultural differences in the environment (Berk, 2017). Sensory experiences not only help develop the brain, but they also promote growth in other areas, or during the windows of opportunity (Myer et al., 2015).

Children who struggle with tasks, such as getting ready to walk, demonstrate these windows of opportunity (Myer et al., 2015). The child may fall to the ground and cry, or an infant getting ready to crawl may just lie on the ground. Educators and parents who recognize these signs can provide encouragement and role models for the child, hold their hands to promote walking, or demonstrate crawling.

Maria Montessori was one of the developmental theorists who wholeheartedly believed in times when children were motivated by certain stimuli and could learn to use them (Gestwicki, 2017). Since children don't alert adults when they are ready to learn, it is the role of the educator and parents to plan an environment that supports growth every day (Myer et al., 2015). Children who do not learn skills when introduced have the ability through reinforcement to have them retaught. Since children learn at their own rates, it is the educator's responsibility to modify and differentiate instruction suitable to the child's learning style (Gestwicki, 2017).

TRAUMA AND BRAIN GROWTH

If part of the cerebral cortex (the largest section of the brain that controls all functions) is damaged, an amazing process occurs. Before the two hemispheres of the cerebral cortex lateralize, the brain has the capacity to change functions due to damage or injuries (Berk, 2017). This is called *brain plasticity* or the ability to take over a function of the brain that was lost from another section of the brain (Berk, 2017; Stuss, 2011). When one area of the brain takes over for another, the area where cells were reduced may show slowness in processing information from the deficit region; thus, educators should become knowledgeable about illness or injuries and develop a plan or learn strategies that promote growth in that region of the brain (Myer et al., 2015).

FINE MOTOR GROWTH

The development of fine motor skills is one of the most critical areas of growth. The ability to hold a pen and write, use a fork to eat, tie shoes, or open a small bottle are all vital components of life. Fine motor development starts from the moment of birth, when an infant touches the mother's skin, and continues throughout the preschool years (Berk, 2017). Well-planned early learning environments give infants, toddlers, and preschoolers the ability to practice fine motor skills by playing with tabletop toys, push beads, rattles, and large blocks; cutting with scissors; and eating with utensils (DeBord, 2016).

Children who don't have the ability to use these advanced skills may need to learn precursor skills; thus, understanding them is necessary for full skill attainment (Carlson, Lelazo, and Faja, 2013). Looking at an infant's hand, for example, one can see that the fingers and palm are quite flat. As the child matures, rounding happens in the hand that allows the child to grasp items such as a spoon or crayon.

To help develop the ability to grasp, not only do the large muscles of the arms have to be formed, but also the smaller muscles in the hand need to be able to move as the child wants them to. If the child tires quickly and complains about his or her arms, the child may need more large-muscle development. Standing at an easel to paint or draw, or using a heavy, wet (with water) paintbrush to paint the side of buildings or fences helps develop the muscles in the chest, arms, and back.

Daily use of Play-Doh, Plasticine, and other stiff mixtures builds the small muscles in the wrist, hand, and fingers (CT ELDS, 2014). Homemade play dough, with many consistencies, promotes the development of both sensory and fine motor skills. Educators, practitioners, and parents may choose to add coffee grounds, oatmeal, sand, or cornmeal to play dough for a different feel. Adding a large assortment of tools for the play dough such as small rolling pins, scissors, and garlic crushers to the play dough table also assists with fine motor skills. Children can stand at the table to use these materials, thus increasing their fine and gross motor development. Kneading bread is an example of how it is easier to stand than to sit when using some muscles.

Learning to reach out for and grasp items should begin as an infant (Berk, 2017). Small rattles, an adult's finger for grasping, squishy noisy toys, pull toys with a short string, and snap beads are all items that are useful in developing fine motor skills. Infants around ten months to a year in age begin to want to hold their own utensils (CT ELDS, 2014). If the handle is too small, the child may not be able to grasp it well. Weighted silverware or utensils with larger handles work well. To make a larger handle, a parent or practitioner may take the spoon handle and slide it through a pop bead. With the bead on it, the grasping area is larger for the child.

For children who have a difficult time grasping items and holding on to them, adding tweezers, turkey basters, and tongs to a sensory table filled with macaroni, beans, sand, or water can be helpful (Peterson, n.d.). Squeezing the turkey baster develops the rounding of the hand for grasping, while tongs promote the use of opposing digits, a precursor for cutting.

Another way to increase fine motor coordination is to take an empty coffee can, cut an X in the middle of the lid, and then put the lid back on the can. The can may be filled with scarves for the child to pull out, or it may be left empty, and the child must push corks through the X (Peterson, n.d.). There are many commercial products that suffice in the classroom, but some of the best items are homemade from recycled materials (CT ELDS, 2015). In an age where budgets are tight and recyclables are plentiful, homemade items take just a few minutes to make and are quite useable.

As toddlers develop manual dexterity, it is time to move on to more difficult items such as small beads for stringing, wiki sticks to make letters, pegs and sticks, lacing, different textured balls, and dressing and shoe frames (Gestwicki, 2017). Many different items can be used to meet the child's goals. The IEP will state the fine motor goal to be accomplished, and it is up to the educator to determine what to use. No matter what the activity or item used, it will most likely provide learning for two or three of the child's goals (Jamison, Forston, and Stanton-Chapman, 2012). Stringing small beads can be used for fine motor dexterity, sorting by shape, and distinguishing colors, size, and patterning. During team meetings, different strategies and materials can be discussed, and parents can imitate and implement some of the same activities at home.

At the preschool age, children can use small tabletop blocks to sort by shape or color, stack by one color, alternate or sequence colors, or use ABA and ABBA patterns (Gestwicki, 2017). Other activities that increase fine motor skills include playing lotto games, where the child has to lift cardboard pieces off the table, playing board games, assembling puzzles, and pouring small containers of rice into a larger container on the sensory table. Another fine motor–development activity uses pennies and requires the child to pick them up one at a time, putting them into the jar using a pincher grip.

Geoboards with rubber bands or a pegboard and golf tees make for a fun group activity to make shapes and letters, write words, and create pictures. Painting upright on an easel or using a slant board helps build both fine and large motor skills. Using different sized brushes helps children to learn control, as do Cray-Pas, large crayons, chalk, and markers (Gestwicki, 2017). Other tools that can be used to increase fine motor skills include fly swatters, small plungers, toothbrushes, combs, picks, bubble wrap made into a mitt, small cars with different treads and different-sized tires, barefoot painting, and finger painting.

From the beginning, children need to learn to hold scissors properly. Novice cutters find that holding their hand upside-down is most comfortable and may be more successful; however, this leads to bad habits. To counter the hand positioning issue, drawing a smiley face on the child's cutting thumb and reminding him or her that "Mommy always needs to be smiling" at the child while he or she is cutting might help. It is vital that the child hold the scissors and paper correctly, turning the paper, not rotating the scissors to cut (Berk, 2017). If the child has difficulty with scissor skills, an occupational therapist can suggest the best strategies linked to the child's special needs.

GROSS MOTOR DEVELOPMENT

Gross motor coordination is a precursor for fine motor development (Berk, 2017). With more children spending time on technological devices, gross and fine motor skills are at a decrease (Rosin, 2013). Sufficient gross motor activities, both indoors and out, improve healthy body image, reduce BMI, and encourage friendships (CT ELDS, 2014). Outside games and activities such as tag, red light/green light, cooperative games, races and obstacle courses, hoops and ball play with assorted ball sizes, riding bikes and scooters (with protective equipment), and using climbers and ladders, as well as swings and rope climbing nets, all develop gross motor skills and, in some cases, fine motor skills.

Other activities that develop gross motor skills include hitting a tennis ball with a badminton racket, kickball racing, walking the plank, learning how to walk on a low balance beam, walking backward, and sliding sideways. To promote hand-eye coordination, practitioners and educators can have children push a large ball, go up and down rope netting, climb stairs, and crawl up and down various surfaces (Gestwicki, 2017; Henniger, 2013).

For children who have limited mobility, full access to the playground with specialized equipment is mandatory. Adaptive swings with a five-point harness system, tire swings with an attached safety seat, and other equipment such as higher sand tables and modified tricycles, as well as an area where a wheelchair-bound but independent child can interact with peers, are must-haves.

ORAL MOTOR DEVELOPMENT

As with all areas of development, each child does so at his or her own rate (Lifter, Mason, and Barton, 2012). Educators may not consider a child's oral motor development in their wheelhouse of responsibility or knowledge; however, oral motor development can be practiced at snack and mealtime, and during outside activities such as bubble blowing and straw painting. Good oral motor health contributes to healthy children and positive brain development (Prado and Dewey, 2014). Any child with diagnosed oral motor delays should be assigned to a speech-language pathologist to oversee treatment.

Depending on the intervention needed, some treatments may be done using a pull-out model, in the classroom or co-treated with other children (Lifter et al., 2012). Speech-language pathologist often co-treat with an occupational therapist since there may be overlaps in treatment protocols (American Speech-Language Hearing Association [ASHA], 2014). The specifics are always outlined in the child's IEP.

Encouraging parents to provide differently textured snacks is ideal to developing oral cavity motor skills, exposing children to different textures, and aiding children with learning appropriate chew patterns. Combining a crunchy cracker, cereal, fresh raw fruit, or vegetable with something soft such as a cheese stick requires the tongue to push food in different directions during tongue lateralization. A wide variety of nutritional snacks and meals promotes good health.

Some children may have to use an internal or external brushing program prior to eating to alert the oral muscles that they need to work (ASHA, 2014); other children may need to be reminded to close their mouth while chewing, take small bites using the front teeth, push the food to the back, allowing it to be chewed, not load the mouth with too much food, and swallow.

All follow-up and directions given to children in the classroom should be under the guidance of a trained professional who is alert to possible choking hazards, overloading of the mouth, and other physical characteristics that may impact eating (ASHA, 2014). All educators, assistant teachers, and paraprofessionals should be trained in first aid, choking, and rescue breathing. Foundations Developmental House (2017) provides a well-populated chart on feeding milestones.

FINAL THOUGHTS

Having excellent fine, gross, and oral motor skills affects other developmental domains and enables the child to take part in everyday and specialized activities. Children develop gross motor skills from head to toe, noted as "cephalocaudal growth," and from the inner trunk to the outside digits, referred to as "proximodistal development." There are specific patterns of development that all children follow; however, birth injuries and developmental delays may change the typical growth progression. Like children, who have sensitive and critical periods of development, educators have opportune times to promote development in their classes.

The dynamic system theory of development uses a combination of complex skills and stimuli to encourage their development. Educators who understand learning progressions and ways to assist and promote children in their classroom use adaptive toys, recyclable materials, and basic interventions in order to have a classroom where children will flourish.

Trauma at birth can cause children to have to use other parts of their brain to replace those neurons that were damaged. *Brain plasticity* is the term used for neurons replacing damaged ones. When this occurs, children may have to learn alternative ways to perform certain functions. The growth progression may be slowed as the cells reformat their original patterns.

Fine and gross motor activities are experiential for both educators and children. Though there are many commercial products that can be bought for programs, the more informal ones made from household goods and recycled materials may also prove to be valuable to the early childhood classroom.

POINTS TO REMEMBER

- *Children's growth progressions may be influenced by their environment, the amount of stimulus received, and by their culture.*
- *Gross, fine, and oral motor skills are important progressions of growth that can be fostered in a well-designed, enriching classroom.*
- *There are both sensitive and critical times of development. Though critical times are important, it is more relevant to understand how to recognize children's sensitive periods and the related windows of opportunity to support, develop, and refine this development.*
- *Plasticity is the brain's ability to transform damaged areas by using other neurons to perform vital movements. Damaged areas may be caused by birth injury or trauma and will require more devoted and specific methods and strategies to develop new areas.*
- *Fine motor activities are plentiful. Educators and parents can share homemade and recycled materials for inclusion in the program materials.*
- *Gross motor activities can be held inside, outside, and in well-equipped playgrounds through group play and games.*
- *Oral motor development is important, as it impacts a child's health and ability to eat and talk.*

Chapter 8

Addressing the Social and Emotional Needs of Young Children

Children learn how to cope in everyday situations from their families, culture, friends, teachers, and communities. Lessons that involve dealing with stress, building self-confidence, developing self-worth, self-regulation, and impulse control all result in the positive development of trusting relationships with adults and other children (Miller, 2016).

Defined in terms of temperament styles, social and emotional development in children falls into specific stages of development and includes the attachment theory (Berk, 2017). Integrated into this development, children learn about the world around them, how to play with others, and about developing appropriate language to get their needs resolved.

BRAIN DEVELOPMENT

Babies are born with more than one hundred billion brain cells that grow rapidly during the months before and immediately after birth. The neurons migrate to their assigned locations, for synapse connections, and as they undergo integration and differentiations (Hanson et al., 2013; Vértes and Bullmore, 2015). The care pregnant mothers receive is vital, as those who have good nutrition, are without stress, and are considered to have healthy pregnancies assist with infantile brain development (Prado and Dewey, 2014).

Teratogens (damaging environmental chemicals, population, disease, or toxins), alcohol, smoking, and stress can have devastating effects on the development of the prenatal brain and are mostly preventable (Lupattelli, Picinardi, Einarson, and Nordeng, 2014). Once babies are born, they need stimulation and adequate nutrition to support brain growth in order to develop attachments and thrive (Galinsky, 2010). The process of *myelination* occurs as a thick white substance develops and becomes an insulation material around the sheath that transmits connections between the neuron's axon and dendrite (Merriam-Webster, 2017).

Teachers and practitioners may think of the sheath as an electric cord that goes between a lamp and the electrical outlet. If there were no covering over the electric cord, the electrical impulses would escape. Myelination provides the cover to each individual neuron, which in turn guarantees that sufficient impulses can travel through the brain (WebMD, 2017).

NEGATIVE FACTORS THAT IMPEDE BRAIN DEVELOPMENT

The first three years of life are the most critical to brain development; however, negative factors can affect its growth: poverty, failure to thrive, family turmoil, few social interactions, constant stress, and environmental hazards are just a few. These stressors raise infants' cortisol level, a stress hormone that can change brain growth patterns. When cortisol remains high, brain growth is compromised (Hanson et al., 2013). Infants need to hear the human voice speaking and singing to them and must experience skin-to-skin touch with a human (mostly with the mother or a caregiver). Infants begin to develop self-regulation and identify with feeling safe early on; therefore, a stress-free environment promotes positive brain growth (Hanson et al., 2013).

DEVELOPMENT OF TEMPERAMENT

Children develop one of three different temperaments (general emotional dispositions): easy/flexible; difficult/feisty; or slow to warm up/fearful (Henniger, 2013). Aspects of temperaments include activity level, task persistence, distractibility, ability to approach, withdrawal, intensity of reaction, and quality of mood (Berk, 2017). Children develop their temperaments and their personality as they traverse Erik Erikson's three stages of social and emotional growth, that include the following:

- **Stage 1: Trust versus mistrust.** Infants under eighteen months who are well attended, have consistency in their life, and a few main caregivers develop trust. If the caregiver is unreliable, inconsistent, and shows no interest in the child, the child develops mistrust.
- **Stage 2: Autonomy versus shame and doubt (eighteen months to three years of age).** The child is developing a sense of trust, able to move away from a main caregiver. A child who explores and manipulates his or her

environment is able to develop a sense of autonomy or independence, self-esteem, and self-control. However, if the caregiver is not supportive and is harsh and condemning, the child will develop self-doubt and may assume that he or she can't act on his or her own. A caregiver should try to find a balance, giving limits and encouragement simultaneously.

• **Stage 3: Initiative versus guilt (three to six years).** Initiative means a positive response to world challenges, taking on responsibilities, learning new skills, and feeling purposeful. Educators should encourage exploration and creativity; this is a time for play, not formal instruction. Children begin to develop a sense of responsibility and guilt. They begin to anticipate the consequences to negative behavior and can feel guilty for an act. This is the beginning of moral judgment (Berk, 2017; Miller, 2016).

SELF-REGULATION

Managing behaviors, working with others, and developing friendships require children to have social and self-regulation skills. These are needed to engage children in the classroom in every learning situation (Merritt, Wanless, Rimm-Kaufman, and Peugh, 2012). Broekhuizen, Slot, van Aken, and Dubas (2016) posit that temperament or children's activity level helps to determine how they develop their ability to attend, calm down, or learn to sit still. Broekhuizen et al. (2016) link cognitive, emotional, and behavioral development to a child's ability to form social and emotional skills, as well as attributing a child's reaction to a situation based on environmental stimuli. Children with difficult or feisty temperaments may react negatively to a stressful environment, whereas an easy-going child has the skills to adjust to it in a positive way (Phillips et al., 2012).

Merritt et al. (2012) make an important observation on how self-regulation affects further learning and the roles early educators play. Children who have positive interactions with educators early in their life develop better self-regulation skills that foster further social growth in elementary school (Broekhuizen et al., 2016). Educators who provide supportive classrooms where interactions are responded to with care and sensitivity observe children who have more sophisticated social and emotional skills. These children become more readily adaptable to changes in their environment by maintaining more acceptable social behaviors (Merritt et al., 2012).

ATTACHMENT THEORY

Harry Harlow (1958) and John Bowlby (1957) are credited with the development of attachment theory. Attachment theory defines the secure psychological long- or short-term interpersonal relationship between two people; it is a bond that connects one person to another, beginning in early childhood, to have needs met (David, 2014; Miller, 2016). Attachment theory describes and explains a collection of "developmental pathways of social-emotional functioning in childhood and adulthood" (Schuengel, de Schipper, Sterkenberg, and Kef, 2013, p. 35) that includes specific behaviors found in close relationships.

Attachment is responsible for the mental and social functioning that is developed in early childhood and is experienced through life by satisfying motivations and needs (Brumariu, 2015; Miller, 2016). When secure attachment does not take place, there may be biologically rooted negative outcomes (Schuengel et al., 2013). Schuengel et al. (2013) have done extensive studies on individuals with intellectual disabilities who have had disrupted attachment through their lifetime and have shown that the well-being of these individuals can be affected in negative ways that then require interventions (Schuengel et al., 2013).

Children who have had secure attachments throughout their life have better emotional development and, therefore, can overcome emotional crises and use adaptive regulation strategies (Brumariu, 2015; Chen and Fleer, 2016). Brumariu's (2015) work has shown that the middle-years' attachment development is critical to emotional and mental regulation as the child's world opens to exploration and negative influences. If bonds deteriorate, then the child may be at risk for poor well-being and unable to make sound moral decisions that would normally protect the person from harm (Schuengel et al., 2013).

HELPING PARENTS DEVELOP A
BOND WITH THEIR CHILD

Educators feel that children come to school already having the perfect bond with their parents; however, in many cases, this is far from the truth. Parents develop a bond with their child during the preschool years, and once the child reaches school, due to complex issues, the bond may not be as strong. Working with a child with a disability may elicit deep-seated, unfavorable feelings from the parents toward their child, or the family may have recently found out their child has a disability, and the parents are still in the grieving process. Furthermore, the parents may be experiencing their own difficult times, impeding their ability to bond tightly with their child.

BENEFITS OF ATTACHMENT TO SOCIAL PLAY

Children who have a secure, meaningful attachment to their parents will be better equipped to participate in social play (Bierman and Motamedi, 2015).

Children who demonstrate the effects of poverty or lack attachments may have a more difficult time in learning social play skills and early language skills, whereas other children will be able to increase their capacities for mental representation and language skills (Hanson et al., 2013). Creating new play opportunities will help children learn to organize their mental capacities about themselves and others (Bierman and Motamedi, 2015).

Play helps to develop language and communication skills through self-discovery. When children interact, or when play is initiated by adults, children learn decision-making and conflict-resolution skills, and better understand the world around them (Merritt et al., 2012; Morena, 2016). Children under four years old are egocentric: they only see the world from their point of view. Peer play helps children develop their skills to view the world through another child's perspective, to make conclusions about what is happening to other people, and to use their language skills to communicate problems to others (Chen and Fleer, 2016; Morena, 2016).

SOCIAL COMPETENCY

Understanding the importance of social competency is significant for parents, and more so for the parent of a child with a disability, who may not have age-appropriate expectations for the child (Zand et al., 2014). Earlier interventions to support social competency benefit children as they work to develop an understanding of others through interactions and to be able to recognize needs and wants.

Interfacing and playing with others and participating in goal-oriented peer activities help children learn hierarchical play skills (Jamison et al., 2012). The hierarchical structure includes a child moving from solitary play to parallel play, then to associative play, and finally to cooperative play (Miller, 2016). These four stages of play are important, as they enable children to recognize and understand social cues and underlying rules, and develop conflict resolution skills and assertive and adaptive strategies to resolve interpersonal conflicts (Filippello, Marino, Spadaro, and Sorrenti, 2013).

STRATEGIES THAT FOSTER SOCIAL
AND EMOTIONAL GROWTH

Environments

Children of any age deserve respectful, encouraging, and warm environments, both at home and at school. It is the educator's responsibility to develop emotionally supportive classrooms (Merritt et al., 2012). Children in classes without well-developed social-emotional skills need differentiated instruction to improve skills. Children with more mature skills can be paired up with those who need extra support (Jamison et al., 2012). Identified children will need more support and most likely will not seek out playmates. Educators can take this opportunity to move a child close to another child with more advanced skills (Jamison et al., 2012).

Classroom staff and materials should mirror the child population. Children feel more comfortable when there are teachers who speak their language and items in the classroom are similar to what they have at home (Jamison et al., 2012). Having pictures that show different emotions hung throughout the classroom enables teachers to quickly help children identify how they are feeling (Vanderbilt University, 2017).

Areas within classrooms or centers should vary between highly active and quiet. Quiet areas give children the opportunity to rest and observe what others are doing in the room (Jamison et al., 2012). Classrooms for second and third graders tend to be more organized to support academic learning, whereas an identified child may need to have more play-based activities. Multipurpose rooms best meet all children's needs.

Cultural Considerations in Play

Children's past experiences influence their knowledge about play and how to interact with others. Cultural experiences predispose children to functioning in the classroom. Educators who understand different aspects of a child's culture will be able to help the child with modifications to the environment and incentives that motivate students. Some children, for example, have learned to wait for the educator to begin play activities, while others use self-initiation (Gestwicki, 2017).

Planning different types of play will benefit children who can make their own decisions. Some children will need more encouragement and "idea placing" by the teacher. Teachers can make suggestions, use PECS (Brody and Frost, n.d.), or use a play sequence that enables children to organize themselves, plan their play, execute it, and then recall or talk about it (HighScope, 2017). Further follow-up in the form of a picture drawn by the child aids in remembering the play and can be used as a communication tool with the parent.

Supporting Different Types of Play

Children with strong problem-solving skills will make friends faster and will be able to model their skills for others. One visual method that helps children develop problem-solving skills is the sunflower method. On flipchart paper, the educator draws a large sunflower with as many petals as there are children in the group; a problem is then written in the center of the sunflower.

Each child gives a solution to the problem, which is written on a petal (Mead, 2017). Under the guidance of the teacher, the children talk about how each solution might work, and they are guided to decide which solution they might try first. That solution is tried for a period of time as determined by the teacher. If the solution doesn't work, another possible one can be tried. Leaving the chart on the wall can be a reminder of the strategy used and the solutions the children are trying (Mead, 2017).

Modeling

Children with disabilities may not be able to watch a role model, internalize the modeling, and mirror the behavior, and instead might require intervention with the help of an adult who demonstrates the behavior on a one-on-one basis. A child who has difficulty entering a play scenario, for example, will need the teacher to model the behavior in order for him or her to understand it (Fleer, 2015; Jung and Sainato, 2013). The teacher might ask the child, "What do you want to do?" This is the first step in helping to define the need. The teacher or practitioner would then repeat back to the child his or her need and ask, "What do you need to do, then?"

If the child is unable to answer the educator, picture boards are helpful tools to illustrate two or three children playing (Lifter et al., 2012). The teacher may give the child language such as "Do you want to play with them?" If the child answers yes, the teacher would ask, "What do you need to ask them?" and then prompt the child with the appropriate language such as, "I want to play." Simple phrases that are repeated in various learning centers will reinforce the skill of entering into play.

Increasing Novel Play

New ideas based on sensory play, large picture big books, alternating between passive and active play, and child-directed and teacher-directed play maintain children's attention and desire to learn (Gestwicki, 2017). Best practice shows that children need downtime to rejuvenate and internalize skills. It is a delicate balance when the IEP is mostly academic. Play and socialization in preschool is paramount to children learning needed skills to be able to proceed to more complicated ones (Shenfield, 2015). Introducing novel ideas keeps a child engaged and learning (Berk, 2017).

Direct Play

This type of play is beneficial for all children, but especially for those who need the steps broken down into discrete parts. Children learn by chunking knowledge, which involves taking smaller chunks of information, tagging them to what is already known, acquiring new thoughts, and consolidating them in the working memory of the brain (Arsaga, 2016).

This strategy is used mostly in a one-on-one situation or a small group of two other children, where the educator recognizes the child's needs and limits the amount of information that can be internalized at one time (Singer, Nederend, Penninx, Tajik, and Boom, 2014). Educators knowledgeable about this strategy have keen insights on what motivates a child, the level of functioning and capacity he or she can organize at one time, and what types of active play are appropriate.

Use of Visuals and Picture Boards

Most children by the age of three can remember two- to three-step directions and sequence the same number of events to make a complete thought. Children who have cognitive learning issues may struggle with completing this task. A visual or PECS (Brody and Frost, n.d.) assists a child in being able to perform a set of activities (ASHA, 2014). For example, typical children know the steps to washing their hands, planning their snack area, eating, and cleaning up, whereas a child who can't sequence the steps requires step-by-step picture cues to find success.

Teaching through Social Stories

The idea of producing social stories as an intervention for children who struggle in social situations was designed by Carol Gray in 1993. Writing stories is a way to reduce or increase desired behavior in a problem situation, as it aids a child in coping, managing, or operating in a situation by giving one solution to a problem (Vickers, n.d.). Since its inception, many educators have taken on the task of designing their own stories, following the guidelines laid out by Gray (Vickers, n.d.). Using social stories in the preschool classroom can help children learn how to interact appropriately, move through transitions calmly, and develop useful personal hygiene.

FINAL THOUGHTS

Positive and healthy development of a child's social-emotional domain is the foundation that supports all other learning and begins before birth. Children who have good skills and understand how to behave in a variety of social situations will be better able to overcome difficulties in life, develop positive relations with others, and develop a respect for human life. Educators who use learning strategies early in a child's life set the child on a positive road for all other challenges that will be forthcoming.

POINTS TO REMEMBER

- *Children learn from the environments they are raised in. Home and school environments that are enriching support positive social and emotional skill development.*
- *Brain development is influenced by proper maternal nutrition while in utero and after a child is born. After birth, positive connections to one or two adults are required for bonding.*
- *Temperament and personality change over time and are molded and modeled by the environment and the adults who impact the child's education.*
- *Eric Erikson's stages of development are valid in understanding how children learn to become functioning adults and contributing members of society.*
- *Caring educators and supportive classroom strategies aid in the development of sophisticated social and emotional skills.*
- *Social play is vital to children learning skills that build self-competency as a way to deal with a myriad of circumstances that they will come in contact with over their lifetime.*

Chapter 9

Speech and Language Delays That Affect Development and Learning

Teachers often describe speech and language development as one component of a child's growth and development; rather, speech and language are
two distinct growth processes that children must develop (ASHA, 2016).
Speech is the use of sounds to make words; a child with a speech disorder
has problems putting together sounds to make words. Language development
is the use of the words to put together thoughts; children with language disorders have problems putting thoughts together (*expressive language*) and/or
have trouble understanding what is being said to them (*receptive language*)
(ASHA, 2016).

Children's ability to articulate sounds to make words and complete
thoughts is vital to developing excellent oral communication skills. Speech
and language developmental issues are some of the most noted delays found
in children under five years of age (Hebbeler and Spiker, 2016). Such delays
impact the ability to make friends, ask and answer questions, and be understood by peers.

LANGUAGE TERMS

Articulation is a child's ability to produce understandable sounds. Some
children will use other sounds as a substitute until a sound can be produced
correctly. This is normal and will correct itself with peer speech models or
an adult modeling the correct sounds; however, by the age of eight, all children should be able to pronounce all sounds (ASHA, 2014). Every classroom
teacher should have available a sound-development chart noting the age at
which children develop sounds. If the child is delayed, then a recommenda-
tion for a screening should follow.

Phonological awareness means words are made up of a sequence of different unit sounds. The minimum word sound is a phoneme; for example, butterfly = but-ter-fly (Core Knowledge Foundation, 2013). *Phonological process* is the ability of a child to produce sound patterns. *Morphology* is the study of the meaning of words and the grammar used (ASHA, 2014). A morpheme is the unit of meaning. *Apraxia* is a motor-speech disorder in which the child knows what he or she wants to say, however, motor coordination or the brain does not allow the muscles of the mouth, tongue, or jaw to form the words (ASHA, 2014).

Stuttering is the prolongation of sounds of speech, usually with the first sound in a sentence. Children often experience disfluency when their minds are working faster than they can produce sounds. Stuttering may happen in tense situations, such as when someone is on the phone or talking in front of a large group (ASHA, 2014).

Semantics is the meaning of individual words, for example, a "block" in a preschool classroom may be a large wooden block, learning blocks with letters or numbers on them, a tabletop set of blocks, or a block of time, as in planning (ASHA, 2014). *Syntax* is the arrangement of words that make a complete thought (Merriam-Webster, 2017). The rules of social language are the *pragmatics* of speech. Pragmatics are governed by culture and within the actual social situation. For children, learning the social rules may take longer when a disability is present, and likewise an adult with a brain injury may not have a solid comprehension of pragmatics (ASHA, 2014).

NORMAL PATTERNS OF LANGUAGE DEVELOPMENT

Infants begin to cry at the time of birth, as they take in their first breath of air and then later to show they are hungry or have discomfort. Before three months of age, infants begin to react to familiar faces and coo back and forth in pre-speech (Berk, 2017). Around this time, an infant may develop a different sound, such as a squeal, that gets reactions from others (ASHA, 2014). Between three and eight months of age, the child begins to babble by making consonant and vowel sounds (Berk, 2017). If reacted to by another child or adult, the baby will continue the sounds. As rudimentary as it is, this is considered the infant's first conversational exchange.

As the baby grows, the sounds the child makes are those that he or she hears on a daily basis (CT ELDS, 2015). Between eight to thirteen months of age, beginning words are spoken, gestures are made and understood, and the child begins to draw attention to objects, labels, and requests (Berk, 2017). By twelve to eighteen months of age, the child may use about fifty words to symbolize objects and ideas and begin to ask for items by pointing or grunting toward an object (CT ELDS, 2015).

During the eighteen-month-to-two-year period in a child's life, two-word sentences or commands are developed and one-step directions are understood (CT ELDS, 2015). The two- to three-year mark brings "word explosions." Though semantics and syntax might not be perfect, children understand the concepts they are talking about and can follow two-step directions (Core Knowledge Foundation, 2013).

Children who are from middle-class to upper-class families ordinarily have a vocabulary of between 1,251 and 2,153 words, whereas children from lower-income families have, on average, fewer than 650 words at age three (Konishi et al., 2014). During the three- to five-year range, children gain at least another 5,000 words, and language becomes a tool for thinking, learning, and organizing themselves (Konishi et al., 2014).

There are several other points about language to consider. Receptive language develops prior to the ability to use expressive speech. Children can understand more than they can express, and the use of nouns develops before verbs (CT ELDS, 2015). Children begin to use morphological markers by adding endings to words that change their meanings; for example, adding "un" to "happy" or changing the meaning of a unit of sound of a word to change its meaning (Berk, 2017).

Between two years to thirty months of age, a child's utterances increase by their adding "ing" and the plural "s." Shortly thereafter, children begin to use pronouns and possessives, though the use may not be totally correct (ASHA, 2014). By three and a half years of age, children use regular past tense and add the articles "a" and "the." Children ages four to five use various forms of "be" and irregular third person forms. These milestones are considered normal development; however, there may be influences that impact typical growth (CT ELDS, 2015).

INFLUENCES THAT AFFECT NORMAL SPEECH AND LANGUAGE DEVELOPMENT

Teachers recognize typical speech and language development but may not have a clear understanding of the developmental situations that contribute to different trajectories of development. Children who are in language-restrictive environments or different cultures may show a decrease in their communication as well as in their social-emotional growth (Escueta, Whetten, Ostermann, and O'Donnell, 2014).

Children who are abandoned or live in homes where conversational language is not used may show a lack of or slowness in their linguistic growth; however, experts feel that children who are adopted between the ages of one and two make strides in language development, assuming a well-supported environment, and that within fifteen months, those children have skills comparable to their typical peers (Escueta et al., 2014).

Glennen (2014) suggests that children who are adopted into homes with middle to high income tend to be supported by well educated parents who recognize the need for a language-rich environment. Adopted children, however, may have trouble developing their syntax and semantics use of language, as they may be affected by their prior culture. This may be in part because in some non-Anglo cultures, the need for play that supports language development is lacking (Lillard et al., 2013). It is imperative, then, that teachers provide strategies for all cultures and families, to include building both teacher and family knowledge about the importance of language development and play.

DUAL-LANGUAGE LEARNERS

Twenty-two percent of US children don't speak English at home, and this figure has doubled in the last thirty years (ACF, 2017c). Many of the children, who are bilingual learners and come from first- and second-generation immigrant families, may also have lower socioeconomic status (ACF, 2017c). Learning two languages has its own sequence of acquisition that must be recognized by educators (Konishi et al., 2014). With more bilingual children enrolled, both education programs and educators need to be well trained in understanding how communication skills develop for a child first learning a language or learning two languages simultaneously (Hoff, 2013).

Quality interactions at home and at school provide the necessary first steps to a positive trajectory. Children who live in homes that are language rich have more sophisticated vocabularies than peers who have not had exposure to language (Hoff, 2013). Classrooms that use dual-language immersion programs with typical and/or atypical children show better results than those with English-only programs (ACF, 2017c; Carlo et al., 2014). A combination of strategies that uses both sensory and social activities builds children's skills (CT ELDS, 2015).

There is a limited amount of data available on children with special needs and the development of language skills; nonetheless, there are adequate strategies that can be used to encourage language development (ACF, 2017c). Educators require knowledge about the second-language acquisition process and how a child's special needs may impact his or her ability to develop linguistic abilities (ACF, 2017c). Teachers who understand the stages of language development or bilingualism show it by providing an appropriate classroom environment that supports children's emotional, social, and behavioral growth. Building these agencies and having positive relationships with children result in acquisition of a new language that meets student-learning goals (CT ELDS, 2015).

PATTERNS OF BILINGUALISM DEVELOPMENT

Children who develop expertise in a second language after having mastered their initial tongue may have different patterns of acquisition (CT ELDS, 2015). These patterns may be affected by the environment the child has been exposed to, language models, and the similarities of the languages such as sounds, vocabulary, and syntax (CT ELDS, 2015). A child learning English, for example, will have trouble in understanding rhymes, as the Spanish language does not utilize rhyming patterns (ACF, 2017c).

Depending on the age of the child, learning two languages requires a period when the child is intentionally listening and is often seen as nonverbal. The child is listening to the sounds that are being used and looking for connections through pictures or human models: for example, telling the child it is diaper-changing time and showing him or her a diaper (Konishi et al., 2014).

The next pattern of development involves children who begin to play with sounds and use words or short phrases to note what they are talking about. Though there maybe multiple errors in the early language patterns, children learn to self-correct by hearing language from others (CT ELDS, 2015). As the next pattern of emergent-speech words increases, the child will be dependent on the context of the situation or materials used to say the proper word, followed by improved fluency. Children in nondemanding social situations can speak freely (CT ELDS, 2015). Due to missing technical and content-specific language, the child may still show errors in semantics and syntax (Core Knowledge Foundation, 2013). The last step in development is fluency, which comes after the child has had opportunities to practice language within multiple contexts (Haynes, n.d.).

RELATIONSHIPS

Children with supportive staff develop relationships built on trust and acquire language skills faster (ACF, 2017c). Children who are newly separated from their parents, in a new school, have special needs, or are learning a second language may feel insecure and scared in their new educational setting. Cultivating secure relationships purposely initiated by educators allows children to develop language more quickly (WIDA, 2014). Children who are in high-quality relationships with adults "encompass features like developing directed speech; adult responsivity to child cues and interests; joint engagement or sharing interest and enjoyment, verbally or nonverbally; and the fluency and connectedness of each conversational exchange" (ACF, 2017c, p. 10).

Children who have strong emotional attachments with caring family members, educators, and others who are important to them develop a sense of belonging that encourages strong language development (CT ELDS, 2015). Relationships use nonverbal gestures to support positive social-emotional development; therefore, a child doesn't need language to develop connections with others. Gestures, facial features, touch, and adults' attending to Maslow's physical comfort levels assist children to make connections between words and meanings (Hoff, 2013). Once the relationship is established and the child feels secure, with no fear of reprisal due to weaknesses in language, the child will be able to further develop his or her skills (CT ELDS, 2015).

SUPPORTIVE LANGUAGE
INSTRUCTION FRAMEWORK

Konishi et al. (2014) posit that children who have supportive language instruction using six evidence-based principles will have increased academic success. In order to increase a child's ability to acquire a second language, these six principles are required: "1: Children learn what they hear most. 2: Children learn words for things and events that interest them. 3: Interactive and responsive rather than passive contexts promote language learning. 4: Children learn words best in meaningful contexts. 5: Children need to hear diverse examples of words and language structures. 6: Vocabulary and grammatical development are reciprocal processes" (Konishi et al., 2014, p. 406).

Children who have intentional conversation with adults while learning a second language acquire more words and link meanings to them faster (ACF, 2017c; Konishi et al., 2014). To increase the frequency at which words are understood and used, linking them to visual items and the spoken word either in English or the child's native language is effective. This strategy works best for an older child who already has a strong repertoire of vocabulary. Children who do not have strong language bases may not be able to link new words to concepts (ACF, 2017c).

Educators must ensure that the contexts in which new words or concepts are introduced are relevant to the child. Children from other countries may not have the foundational knowledge to relate to concepts being taught; rather, educators should check the child's foundational knowledge first through bilingual instruction before adding concepts that are new to the child (CT ELDS, 2015). Engaging relational members to assist with the assessment of knowledge a child possesses is helpful and stresses the importance of family involvement (Mapp, 2014). Children under five years of age are often intrigued by sensory experiences such as playing with rice, sand, play dough, and other sensory mediums. These mediums can be used for children to learn terms about a variety of adjectives, such as soft, hard, cold, hot, bumpy, smooth, and so on (CT ELDS, 2015).

Active interactions rather than passive activities encourage language development. Face-to-face and eye contact develop language. Experiences that work well include taking turns blowing "raspberries" or cooing back and forth with infants, short conversations with older children, listening to directions, or a game meant to develop language skills. Interacting with other children helps to scaffold and increases word usage (Konishi et al., 2014). While some would assume that the use of computers, televisions, or tablets would increase the speed of language acquisition, it is actually the opposite and has the potential to slow down the process of learning.

Children who use words in meaningful environments make language connections faster. Meaningful environments are those places where children can practice their life skills, for example, the housekeeping area, block-building table, or social play outside. When children set the table, pretend to eat a meal or snack, wash the dishes, or operate a microwave or vacuum cleaner, they are learning self-help skills in which language learning comes more naturally (Konishi et al., 2014). Children with disabilities may need picture boards to understand the sequencing of an activity, as well as an adult who verbalizes the steps. Both methods begin to pattern the activity in a child's brain, and connections in the brain are patterned for language use (ACF, 2017b).

Children learning a second language, as well as atypical children, learn best when there are multiple sources of language input. Communication from both male and female voices helps children to develop phonemic awareness or the differentiation of sounds. As children begin to understand the meaning of a word, the context of the meaning should be expanded. Pointing out the *bear* in a storybook helps a child to understand it is an animal. Later, when a child is asked to put socks on his or her *bare* feet, the child is learning another meaning to the word. At this point, language acquisition does not include the child's understanding the meanings of the different spellings, unless the child is older.

As children learn the syntax of language, they may use one word for another in their original language. This is called code switching. For children who are dual learners, in conversations, they will switch a term from the stronger language to fill in for an unknown word (Hammer et al., 2014).

Language and grammar are learned together; they cannot be learned separately (Konishi et al., 2014). As children learn new words, they play with the way they sound and listen to how adults model words correctly. By listening and trying out new sounds, children self-correct; thus, role models using correct grammar and speech are vitally important. Educators who use proper English and understand the needs of dual-language learners will have children who learn to speak the dominant language of the school quickly, regardless of other factors (Konishi et al., 2014).

CLASSROOM STRATEGIES

Speech Articulation

Strategies used by speech-language pathologists can benefit all children. A simple suggestion to increase speech articulation may include snacks that are crunchy, tough to chew, or varied in texture, as they can increase oral muscular-skeletal development. Blowing through and drinking with straws help form the lip muscles and increase airflow (ASHA, 2014). Blowing cotton balls across a table during playtime or blowing bubbles outside increases the ability to feel where the lips are to produce airflow.

Diet

A child's diet can affect the ability to rotate food in the mouth. A child who has a soft, mushy diet may learn a different type of chew pattern by slurping soft, flowable liquids. This affects the child's ability to form sounds and to have clear articulation patterns. Children whose intake includes raw, crunchy foods use better chew, rotate, and swallow patterns (ASHA, 2014).

Conversations

Children learn conversation skills based on the words they hear and the richness of adult interactions. Children who hear vocabulary words that are used within their knowledge base have a better command of words and are then able to engage in more complex conversations (Hebbeler and Spiker, 2016). When children have therapy sessions with a speech-language pathologist (S-LP), it is advantageous for children to be treated individually rather than in group settings. It benefits educators if they are able to attend a therapy session or speak with the S-LP, as they can learn strategies to assist the struggling child. Most service providers are willing to share expertise, as it benefits all the children in the class.

Increase Music and Singing

Children learn new sounds by practicing them. Songs such as "Willoughby Wallaby Woo" by Raffi teach alliteration by changing the first sound of the word (Raffinews, 2017). Discrete hearing of sounds helps children differentiate them to be able to make new words and to develop phonemic awareness.

Singing aids children in developing speaking cadence and intonation; this becomes a basis for reading.

Music and Movement

Gardner's Multiple Intelligences Paradigm stresses that each child has a modality that is best employed for learning (Young and Celli, 2014). Children who learn through bodily-kinesthetic and musical intelligences, for example, like body and physical movement, dance and learn best through music. Educators who recognize the learning styles design curricula and use strategies that improve children's outcomes (Young and Celli, 2014).

FINAL THOUGHTS

Understanding the patterns of speech and language development and language terms is important when working with speech-language pathologists. A pathologist's deep understanding of methods that work to enhance children's ability can be shared with educators for generalization in the classroom. Educators should also consider the environments that children have lived in, the type of experiences they were engaged in, and the expectations from families to develop speech and language.

With more children immigrating to the United States who are dual-language learners, it is important for educators to be well versed in the discrete stages of language development. Understanding second-language acquisition and the experiences that children bring with them aids teachers in planning strategies to enhance development. Providing effective language models in the classroom and at home, if possible, will help children develop as dual-language learners.

Relationships that children develop, both at home and in school, that are socially based help them quickly acquire the necessary skills for further learning. Strong relationships provide children with a sense of belonging that prompts higher degrees of speech and language development. Konishi et al. (2014) use six evidence-based principles to assist children to develop language. The principles, when employed in the classroom, provide educators with a framework for language acquisition.

POINTS TO REMEMBER

• *There is a distinct difference between language and speech development. Speech development deals with articulation of the words, while language deals with how words are put together to makes complete thoughts.*

- *Understanding terms used in speech and language acquisition aids educators in working closely with pathologists.*
- *Dual-language learners have a unique sequence of acquisition skills, and dual-language programs show better academic outcomes regardless of whether students are typical or atypical.*
- *Patterns of language development vary due to the environments children have experienced and whether the child lives in a literacy-rich environment.*
- *Educators who use multiple strategies and the principles of language development (Konishi et al., 2014) will observe that dual-language students excel.*

Chapter 10

Potency of Play as an Intervention

Play is defined as: participating in an activity not for a practical purpose, but rather for enjoyment (Merriam-Webster, 2017). Gestwicki (2017) defines play as a task that is easy to accomplish, has a valuable purpose though undefined to the child, and is self-motivated and process oriented, while others add that play helps build all developmental domains (Berk, 2017; Lillard et al., 2013).

Play is one of the best defining behaviors that children engage in that advances all the development domains (Gestwicki, 2017). Play teaches children how to make sense of the world, try out their own rules on others, discover solutions to tough problems, and create their own knowledge (CT ELDS, 2015). Play is the primary context in which children learn socialization and how to react to others and develop social awareness and acceptance (Stanton-Chapman and Brown, 2015).

Wood and Hall (2011) define play as children's learning to understand their social and cultural worlds, the role each plays during interactions, cooperation, and problem solving. Though the definition has changed little throughout the years, it remains educators' responsibility to intentionally provide enough play-based activities to foster well-rounded development (Jung and Sainato, 2013). Play should be designed so that it helps bring self-directed joy to children. Children who show delight in working with other children or learn new skills through cooperative and associative play develop "independence, self-confidence and problem-solving skills" (CT ELDS, 2015, n.p.).

To better understand the milestones of play, numerous theorists such as Vygotsky, Erikson, and Piaget designated the stages of play development that normally developing children traverse through (Gestwicki, 2017; Miller, 2016; Wood and Hall, 2011). The stages of play provide an intellectual understanding of, and expectations in, preschool classrooms; however, over the past thirty years, pundits (Mead, 2017; Miller, 2016; Wood and Hall; 2011) suggest that the concept of stages is not totally useful, as there is not consideration for "a contemporary interpretation of sociocultural theories" (Stanton-Chapman and Brown, 2015, p. 268). With multiple cultures represented in the classroom, a global definition that is inclusive of cultural contexts is required to meet the needs of all children in a preschool special education classroom (Berk, 2017; Mead, 2017).

The IDEA regulations mandate that most of a child's day be with typical peers and in the least restrictive environment (LRE) (IDEA, n.d.). Pull-out programs have the potential to minimize the time that atypical children have to learn how to play individually, with peers and under the guidance of an educator. Families from several foreign countries do not practice the Anglo belief about imaginary play, and children who have disabilities ordinarily don't have much self-directed playtime (Berk, 2017; Davis-Temple, Jung, and Sainato, 2014; Lillard et al., 2013). With the number of children who have autism spectrum disorder and ADHD rising, the need to teach social skills at an early age is imperative (American Psychiatric Association, 2016; CDC, 2014; Hirsch, 2016).

Through play, typical children move from concrete concepts to the understanding of abstract concepts; however, atypical children may have problems understanding the nuances of play and how it affects their ability to excel in the social sphere (CT ELDS, 2015; Gestwicki, 2017). Moving from a context-based free play to a more structured curriculum that meets the mandates of state and national polices is problematic for some schools (Wood, 2013). Wood (2013) stresses that teachers may be interpreting the signals that children send about their interests of play contexts inappropriately and/ or teachers are ignoring cultural nuances (Gestwicki, 2017) or lack the ability to identify with them.

Culture determines the play environment, what materials are provided, whether individual or group peer play, and the level of interaction a supportive adult maintains (Berk, 2017; Gestwicki, 2017). Adults facilitate play by becoming a play partner or a teacher of direct instruction. Although both approaches may work with children, a deep dive into play exposes that children learn skills best when the environment is supportive, with a facilitating adult rather than one who directs the play, thus learning through experiential-based curriculum rather than play-based experiences (Woodrow, 2014).

The use of television, touch screens, and computers has had detrimental effects on associative and cooperative play (Gestwicki, 2017; Masur, Flynn, and Olson, 2015; Rosin, 2013). From the time Jane Healy wrote the book *Endangered Minds: Why Children Don't Think and What We Can Do about It* (1999) to today, there has been considerable controversy over the use of technology and its detrimental effects on play.

Healy coined the term *zombie effect*, that of children hypnotized by screen time, causing negative effects to their development (Rosin, 2013). Children who watch television for long hours do not show positive growth effects or learn the socially relevant information that hands-on play incorporates (Troseth, Russo, and Strauss, 2016). Without a doubt, the value of face-to-face contact far outweighs any growth shown by long-term exposure to technology (Troseth et al., 2016).

For children with special needs, direct instruction or learning through play has been the route that many teachers employ to educate their students. Notwithstanding the delivery of instruction, Gestwicki (2017) posits that time for normal play be provided for students who use reinforcing play materials. Modifications can be made, since many children with special needs may not self-initiate play.

The Council for Exceptional Children (2017) advocates providing extended time for play, as it is essential to a child's development. Pretend play is valuable to all children in an inclusive environment by providing modifications and affording children with severe needs to advance other developmental domains. Higher levels of complex play that cannot be accomplished through free play can be experienced with adult facilitation (Barton and Smith, 2015).

PLAY AS AN INTERVENTION

Children with typical skills ordinarily engage in play, and through it, learn how best to work with others, respond to affective cues, and sustain their play, whereas children with atypical developmental patterns struggle with making friends, sustaining play, and gaining any depth to their interactions (Gestwicki, 2017; Jung and Sainato, 2013). Children with specific diagnoses such as autism may display behaviors that are not conducive to encouraging group play. It is through modeling and purposeful play that children develop social skills; thus, having one or two adults who lead and assist to hone play skills helps the child become more confident (Shenfield, 2015).

An adult often determines the quality of play children experience by setting up the environment and deciding how to approach it. Educators who look at their students and see the child's disability often use a deficits approach. Allyn and Morrell (2016) suggest using a strengths-based approach to better serve children in developing their play skills.

Teachers who have observed children know their abilities and can "reframe the child's understanding of him/herself from a deficit understanding to an empowerment understanding is a crucial move" (Allyn and Morrell, 2016, p. 129). Educators can extend the child's ability to learn by using supportive phrases such as, "I admire you when you . . . . I noticed that you . . . . It makes me proud when you . . . or I want to compliment you for . . . ." (Allyn and Morrell, 2016, p. 129). For children with developmental delays, other language may need to be used to extend the play so that it reflects the intent of the earlier phrases.

Play has traditionally been thought of as an activity that the teacher observes as opposed to one in which she or he participates. While one researcher argues that it is acceptable to move into child's play and, in fact, be the play partner, another advocates that educators refrain from interrupting, thereby giving children the time and space to problem solve and develop their own style of play (Allyn and Morrell, 2016; Fleer, 2015).

Adults may be responsible for developing themes and enhancing children's play for atypical students or for those who have not had the experience to develop their own skills. Children should be allowed to struggle, as that is how they learn. Children, typical or atypical, will most often find solutions when they push through a difficult situation, assuming they have been given the tools to solve the struggle.

Assuming that all children have the ability to learn, Fleer (2015) posits that understanding play pedagogy is actually a representation of Vygotsky's cultural-historical theory. This theory shows that children have the ability to be a main character in culturally relevant play themes while being outside the play in such roles as gathering materials (Fleer, 2015). This results in the teachers' role becoming central to students developing their imaginary and creative play skills (Hakkarainen, Bredikyte, Jakkula, and Munter, 2013). This premise is contrary to thoughts Allyn and Morrell (2016) reveal about giving space for children to learn. These two opposing viewpoints can become the basis of a rich discussion that teachers can have about their own beliefs and teaching pedagogies.

Play scenarios or "playworlds" (Fleer, 2015) attribute their success in building children's skills with teachers who are intimately engaged, provide materials, read a key story to begin play, and/or give advice on roles (Bredikyte, 2011; Fleer, 2015). Playworlds were originally developed in Sweden and support children in collective play roles that solve dramatic problems, which are defined as "adult-child joint play activities inspired by Vygotsky's theories of play, art and imagination" (Ferholt and Rainio, 2016, p. 1) through co-construction. Being in close proximity to the play allows teachers to be able to sustain the play, pick up story roles when they begin to falter, and support collective activities (Fleer, 2015; Gestiecki, 2017; Singer et al., 2014).

It is well documented that children with learning needs require accommodations within the classroom, through the school and outside of the traditional learning environment, as a way to meet developmental goals (CT ELDS, 2015; Gestwicki, 2017; Leffel and Suskind, 2013). IDEA states that reasonable accommodations must be made for all children with special learning needs, resulting in environments and instruction that all can access. In the case of play, it may require breaking down the steps, adapting materials, and helping the child develop a vested interest (Gestwicki, 2017; U.S. Dept. of Education, n.d.b).

A child who is deaf, partially deaf, or has cochlear implants, for example, needs to be seated near a teacher, who may repeat what another says, while being able to directly see the speaker, or the speaker may be asked to use a device that directs the voice more clearly to the child (Diehl and McFarland, 2012). With other children, a rudimentary attempt at signing may supplement communication between two people, as would formal signing between children and adults (CT ELDS, 2015; Diehl and McFarland, 2012).

Teacher strategies enhance student learning and can be tailored to the needs of each child. The Connecticut Early Learning Developmental Standards (CT ELDS, 2015) list strategies such as acknowledge, model, facilitate, support, scaffold, co-construct, demonstrate, and direct. The strategies go from indirect to direct instruction. Children with disabilities will move toward meeting milestones, and their development will increase with targeted strategies (CT ELDS, 2015). These strategies are not only useful in supporting play but also any interactions with children. Direct intervention, such as co-constructing, demonstrating or directing instruction, has the most value with most children with communication deficits (Stanton-Chapman and Brown, 2015).

HighScope's (2017) "plan-do-review" approach uses three distinct processes to develop a child's executive functioning. In small groups, teachers and children plan what they would like to do. Children become the active learners, while the teacher remains the facilitator and observer. Children verbalize the planning in terms of materials and what they will do. The next step engages children in actively executing their plan, and then, with the guidance of the teacher, the children review what they did (HighScope, 2017). Often, this can be accomplished by a child making a drawing of what he or she did, or by an older child writing about what he or she did. Either way can show the steps the child takes and what the child learned from them.

Children's ability to learn executive functioning through play increases their ability for later learning. Executive functioning is development that takes place in the prefrontal cortex during early childhood that enables the brain to think, act, integrate new information to solve problems, and format sequences of activities, and for the child to go through life having a plan to execute necessary functions (Carlson, Lelazo, and Faja, 2013). Executive functioning includes choosing and planning activities, task persistence, cognitive flexibility and working memory, and regulation of attention and impulses.

Play assists in choosing and planning activities and task persistence. A child who uses the plan-do-review sequence, along with a visual schedule, for example, will develop lifelong executive functioning skills (HighScope, 2017). Using visuals as a sequencing tool, the child learns how to put his or her socks and shoes on or how to use a tool in a play environment by dressing a doll. Perhaps a child learns to manipulate puzzle pieces by turning the pieces repeatedly until they fit in the puzzle (task persistence) (CT ELDS, 2015).

Accommodations throughout play are required so that all children who have access problems are included in like activities. A child in a wheelchair, for example, may have a small bucket of sand on the chair's tray (Dominica, 2015; Watson, 2017). Other children may be paired up with the wheelchair-bound student so they can play together, and the child can participate in the activity.

For some children, travel from one activity to another may be tiring. A child who has leg braces, for example, may not be able to walk to the gym on the other side of the building. Providing a wagon and allowing a friend to tag along may give that child a greater desire to access the gymnasium. These accommodations are true examples of providing supports that enable a child to fully participate with typical peers.

To increase engagement in play, teachers who are aware of the children's needs will design environments that provide physical access to everyone. As teachers move from an indirect role to a more direct role in children's play, being able to access all areas comfortably will increase student skills (Humphries and Rains, 2017). Another strategy may include a picture or communication board that helps a child understand how to begin engagement in an area. These boards are used to reinforce everyday skills and structure an environment that supports learning (Humphries and Rains, 2017). A board in the play area might show the play sequence as: find a friend, lead the friend to the play area, and so on.

No matter what the boards are called (*sequence*, *visual*, or *communication* boards), they provide struggling children with a clear understanding of what comes next, using a visual representation (Humphries and Rains, 2017). In classrooms where students move at the speed of light, a child with sensory issues, special learning needs, or autism may find the environment too stimulating to be able to process next steps. Boards are a way to help the child organize him- or herself, see the next steps, and tune out the surrounding world to be able to accomplish a task (Humphries and Rains, 2017).

Teachers play many roles within the classroom that encourage children to play. Three powerful interactions are necessary for the teacher who is attuned to the needs of students (Dombro, Jablon, and Stetson, 2011). The educator must connect with children by letting them know they are there, the adult must help them make friends and solve problems, and last, the teacher is there to extend their learning (CT ELDS, 2015; Gestwicki, 2017). Extending their learning is a teacher's primary responsibility. After educators are able to provide powerful interactions, they will be able to use strategies to increase student learning.

Problem Solving During Play

The HighScope approach uses a six-step process as defined by Evans (2016). The steps acknowledge that children have conflicts and can use solutions to try to resolve them. Step 1 is to stop any harmful language or behavior by being calm and understanding. Step 2 acknowledges the feelings of both parties, talking through how they feel, followed by Step 3, asking each child what is happening.

In the third step, the adult must gather information, while in Step 4, the educator restates the problem, ensuring that he or she has it right and the children agree with it, and (Step 5) asks for possible solutions. After a solution is determined, the educator then supports the solution (Step 6) and provides follow-up.

The many roles that educators play are vital to all children's success. From planning the classroom to role-playing in the housekeeping area, educators' skills to extend play through modeling, coaching, and scaffolding are fundamental for children's learning. Teachers who use modeling and coaching help children learn strategies in problem solving, investigating hypotheses, and working through situations (Snyder, 2017). An example of this is that Child A has an IEP goal of learning problem-solving skills by being paired with a competent Child B under the coaching of a teacher.

The scenario might play out like this in the block area: The children are laying out blocks flat on the carpet, and the teacher realizes that Child A is not building upright structures. Child B places two blocks upright; one is longer than the other. Child A repeats the same thing while Child B tries to add a top to it, but the structure falls down. The teacher places two sets of the same-size blocks upright. Both children take blocks and put them on top; the structure becomes stable. The teacher then watches the children repeat the activity numerous times, adding other adjoining structures to the original one. The teacher helps Child A talk about what he or she is doing, which helps the child internalize the newly learned skills (Snyder, 2017).

LINKING PLAY AND LANGUAGE DEVELOPMENT WITH LITERACY EXPERIENCES

Language development is paramount to pretend play. Children try out words with others, identify meanings with symbols, and use materials in creative play to represent another item or symbolic play (Lillard et al., 2013). Sadly, only five out of sixteen non-Anglo homes value play, and many other cultures think of play in very different terms (Berk, 2017). This statistic shows the need to educate parents about the importance of play and to give children the opportunity to play, an activity that they may not be regularly exposed to (Lillard et al., 2013).

Under the guidance and keen observations of an educator, examples can be shared with parents that reinforce the value of play and help parents to understand the benefits of what the child is doing during the school day. Educators who link emergent curricula to literacy experiences will observe an increase in the use of new words, and the children's play skills will become richer.

FINAL THOUGHTS

Play is defined as a task that is easy to accomplish, has a valuable purpose though undefined to the child, and is self-motivated and process oriented (Gestwicki, 2017). Play helps build all of the developmental domains (Berk, 2017; Lillard et al., 2013). With adult support, play skills are easy to develop in all children, including those with disabilities and who need adaptations and modifications.

Styles of play and parental beliefs impact the type of play children engage in. Cultures also determine whether cooperative or solitary play is encouraged. Technology has certainly changed how cooperative and associate play has developed. With more children spending large amounts of time playing by themselves, there is a decrease in group playtime that has led to fewer peer problem-solving skills and less cooperative play.

All children can learn effective play skills, and providing accommodations and modifications to the classroom supports children who learn differently and who may have physical limitations. Adapting environments for full access and using strength-based play strategies enhance a child's ability to learn new skills. The HighScope (2017) curriculum endorses educator facilitation and observation with children's play, and information gathered supports the next steps to increase student competency.

Executive functioning is learned through play by problem solving, deciding next steps, and making new synapses in the brain. Play-based programs that encourage literacy and language development show promise in increasing children's vocabulary and ability to communicate. Educators who share the value of play and help parents understand its importance observe children who make friends quickly and have the skills necessary for future learning.

POINTS TO REMEMBER

- *The value of play is viewed differently based on a family's culture.*
- *Educators play important roles in making accommodations to learning environments and modifications to play items so that all children have full access.*
- *Technology has had detrimental effects on learning cooperatively and associative play.*
- *HighScope provides a framework to enhance play.*
- *Executive functioning is learned through play, and it is the educator's responsibility to promote its use.*

Chapter 11

Critical Transitions
Moving Forward after Preschool

Critical transitions for our youngest children and families can pose difficult challenges. Children can be identified at any time as needing special education services. Transitions that children go through when they are identified during their first three years may require lengthy services. For children under the age of three, an Individualized Family Service Plan, or IFSP, is developed that focuses largely on the inclusive needs of the families and on their children's development in all domains. The IFSP is governed under IDEA, Part C, in most cases in a home or natural environment, and is family centered (Podvey et al., 2013).

When a child turns three, services transition to the school district in which the child lives. The child's Individual Education Plan, or IEP, developed under the mandates of IDEA, Part B, now focuses on the educational needs of the child and will benefit the student's academic achievement in school. In most cases, services are delivered in an inclusive preschool classroom or individualized therapy room under the guidance of an occupational or physical therapist or speech-language therapist (Hebbeler and Spiker, 2016).

As early as two and one half years of age, the transition process may begin to prepare the family for the public preschool program. The advance time before the child turns three is helpful for preschool planning teams' needs and to offer the families time to decide on programming and wraparound care for their child if full-time care is needed.

SUPPORTING FAMILIES AS THEY TRANSITION TO PRESCHOOL-BASED PROGRAMMING

Transitioning from a home environment to a center-based one is often perplexing for families. Service delivery is different from what families have

111

been accustomed to, and instead of one-on-one and exceptionally small settings, the delivery of services is offered in a larger setting and educationally focused, as required by IDEA, Part B. The change in settings requires that supportive links between program ideals and families be created, and often educators are the ones to help facilitate these relationships (Podvey et al., 2013).

When families and their children transition from a family-centered program to an academic program, the first difference often noticed is the learning environment (Podvey et al., 2013). The learning environment or classroom may feel more sterile than that of a home environment and is usually larger, and parents often find that the number of people and multiple concurrent activities make it feel chaotic. In actuality, the reverse is true: each person in the room has a specific role, children to attend to, and IEP goals to accomplish (Podvey et al., 2013). Aiding parents to understand the new environment, its distinct purpose, and how staff work harmoniously is often daunting but is necessary to help make families feel comfortable.

Transitioning children from a home-based environment to a preschool program requires attending to children who may not yet know how to make and play with friends and lack experience with problem solving, conflict resolution, and knowing how to get their needs met (Hebbeler and Spiker, 2016). Service providers such as the OT, PT, and S-LP will change at this point, which often makes the transition more difficult (Podvey et al., 2013). Showing compassion, listening to families, and giving suggestions and feedback helps comfort the families and often makes the transition easier.

Parents can be supported by educators who take time to explain the mechanics of the classroom by encouraging them to look for different experiences that children are having, and how each area in the room provides opportunities for their child's goals to be met (Gestwicki, 2014). Parents who are able to take the time to intentionally visit the program several times before the child is in attendance will build a better understanding of the program, which makes the transition easier for both the child and the family.

Another challenge for families is a feeling of losing control over all decisions made for their child and in the execution of services. Though the IEP process takes into consideration educational concerns families have, the way services are implemented may be contrary to what is familiar to parents (Podvey et al., 2013). Implementation of services is delivered without daily family interactions; however, daily communication as to how the child is responding to treatments and other interventions will help parents feel that they are part of daily school interactions.

Parental values are often the root cause of these concerns. Parents may question the alignment of their family beliefs to those of a more formalized setting (Podvey et al., 2013; Powers, 2016). Helping parents develop an understanding of the child's program and how it is aligned to family values is an important asset that educators can learn to have. Strategies that connect what the child is tasked with to the child's educational goals, and explaining how decisions are made linked to the child's treatment-based, evidence-based practices, will be most effective.

To counter the negative effects transitions can pose, having clear understandings between educators, schools, and families is paramount before families begin a program (Powers, 2016). Outside of the IEP process, many special education teachers implement joint team meetings between the child's teacher, support staff, and parents. The team meetings emphasize strategies that are and will be used with the child, and how they can be supported both at home and in school. Parents who feel they are part of this process realize quickly that they are indeed still in control of their child.

CHALLENGES OF MEANINGFUL INCLUSION PROGRAMS: BLENDED PRESCHOOL CLASSROOM

Blended preschool classrooms housed in preschools, childcare centers, and public and private schools are mandated by the American with Disabilities Act (U.S. Dept. of Justice Civil Rights Division, 1990) to make accommodations that are reasonable to enable all children to participate (Crisalli, 2016). The ADA ensures that children of all abilities can participate in all preschool programs. Each program must complete an assessment to meet the needs of the child without fundamentally changing the program (IDEA, n.d.). There are other factors of ADA that need to be taken into consideration before a child is not allowed into, or expelled from, a program (Crisalli, 2016). It is suggested that programs consult with local ADA experts to identify the parameters that the program must operate under.

Programs can use community resources to meet the needs of children and work with families and service providers to make accommodations and to provide teacher training, if necessary. Educators who question their abilities, or simply want to acquire a stronger knowledge base, can learn from S-LPs, OTs, and PTs the strategies that are specific to the children in the classroom. Local educational and community programs may offer further education on working with children with special needs through professional development opportunities.

Educators may demonstrate low self-efficacy in their teaching practices and classroom management techniques (Park, Dimitrov, Das, and Gichuru, 2014). Educator perception of efficacy to serve children with disabilities affects their attitudes and those who work with them. When teachers perceive that they have high self-efficacy, they employ more effective behavioral and classroom management practices (Park et al., 2014). Nevertheless, teachers with little self-efficacy may use little effort, as they don't believe they are effective with the strategies they use. Teachers who believe they are too poorly educated to work in inclusive classrooms have opportunities to improve their education through formal college coursework, and other informal training, such as communities of practices.

Those who have high self-efficacy are more motivated to put forth effort to seek out other strategies that make a difference for the students in their class (Park et al., 2014). It has been shown that the ability to collaborate with other preschool teachers, rather than function within classroom silos, enables educators to share strategies, improve practice, and deal with difficult circumstances by learning together. Gibson and Dembo's (1984) Teacher Efficacy Scale, Hoy and Woolfork's (1993) Teacher Efficacy Scale, and Sharma, Loreman, and Forlin's (2012) Teacher Efficacy for Inclusive Practices (TEIP) are all tools that educators and staff can use to move toward a more professional practice.

Mainstreaming

The reauthorization of IDEA (n.d.) includes more specific language on the term "least restrictive environments" and a redetermination of time spent in regular classrooms. This can become an issue for mainstream teachers whose teacher-preparation programs lacked the educational components for integrating children with disabilities (Hamilton-Jones and Vail, 2014). Teacher-preparation programs should include pedagogical knowledge about strategies of working with atypical children and working with families, and the benefits of inclusion and building collaborative relationships (Mapp, 2014; Podvey et al., 2013).

Hebbeler and Spiker (2016) question whether teacher-preparation programs prepare educators well enough to use mainstreaming and specific instructional practices in an integrated or mainstreamed classroom. Regular education teachers may struggle with understanding all the requirements in an IEP or 504 plan (Hamilton-Jones and Vail, 2014). The IEP clearly defines what accommodations are required to be made within the room for the child's education plan and the goals the child is expected to achieve, while the 504 plan defines what accommodations are required to be made to the child's academic plan.

Though the IEP clearly defines the goals relevant to the child's progress, strategies that are effective may take time to develop in teachers just beginning to work in an integrated classroom (Hamilton-Jones and Vail, 2014; Hebbeler and Spiker, 2016). Inexperienced teachers mentored by veteran teachers benefit from learning strategies and techniques that are effective with all children (Hebbeler and Spiker, 2016).

Accommodations and the Learning Environment

Accommodations in both an IEP and a 504 plan for the inside environment often include preferential seating, screened work areas, larger work spaces, slant boards, modifications to timed tests, transportation assistance between areas within the school, different lighting, and large-print books. Outdoor and playground accommodations include hard surfaces for playground access for children with walking disabilities or those using a wheelchair, different types of swings for children with physical limitations that have a five-point harness, and higher, elevated sandboxes and water tables (Dunst, Trivette, Hamby, and Simkus, 2013). Other accommodations may include those for increased bathroom use, feeding assistance, and rest periods built into the day.

The learning environment may contain adaptive equipment and other equipment that meets the needs of children requiring wheelchairs, standers, feeding trays and weighted balls, vests, and blankets (Dominica, 2015). Other features of the classroom that assist atypical children are larger management-system boards, adaptive furniture for circle time, specific chairs for proper seating, computers with larger screens, and large areas in the room to accommodate wheelchairs and children with mobility issues (Watson, 2017). Other adaptive equipment, whose function teachers may need to explain to parents, includes switch interface devices, powered mobility devices, and augmentative communication devices (Dunst et al., 2013).

Parents may think that equipment use in an inclusive setting might be detrimental or distracting to their child's program or dangerous to their child. It is the educator's responsibility to explain how these accommodations make the classroom inclusive for all children, and how their child benefits from an inclusive classroom. Parents may question whether their child will regress by being in a classroom with atypical children or if the child will emulate inappropriate behaviors displayed by others. Educators can carefully explain that children do learn from others, though most children learn to be caring and compassion when in inclusive classrooms.

TEACHING STRATEGIES

Teaching strategies target certain behaviors or delays that are prevalent in some classrooms, while other classrooms are more child centered, and teachers follow the lead of the children. The reason for the difference is often the degree of support the child needs, based on his or her IEP. Inclusive classroom strategies can be more general and adaptable to more students, making the room more child centered. In self-contained rooms, the teaching strategies are more child specific and tailored personally to each individual student's needs.

Educators in some classrooms may rely on peers, as a teaching strategy, to model behaviors that are reinforced by the lead educator (Hebbeler and Spiker, 2016). It is the hope of educators that children with disabilities will generalize skills as quickly as typical children do, but they often find that atypical children need more targeted instruction reinforced over time for skill development (Gestwicki, 2017).

Least Restrictive Environment

IDEA requires that children with disabilities spend time in the least restrictive environment and with typical peers; therefore, preschool programs maintain a 50 percent ratio of typical to atypical children (IDEA, n.d.). The time prescribed for services identified in the child's IEP must remain constant, so careful planning by educators is required to adhere to the IDEA requirements. Typical children are chosen to be role models and play models for other children and being with them provides time for identified children to be mainstreamed with like-aged peers.

With 753,697 children ages three to five receiving special education services under IDEA, helping parents understand the purpose behind an inclusive classroom and the benefits that their child will gain becomes imperative (U.S. Department of Education, 2014). For some families, the reduced fee attracts them to the program; however, they may have little understanding of the philosophy of the program. Schools use playgroups to identify appropriate peers and to describe inclusive programming. Being able to thoroughly describe the program is advantageous for consistency of enrollment of the children and the development of an individualized curriculum that affects each child (IDEA, n.d.).

Children with severe disabilities who require one-on-one services may be assigned to a self-contained classroom. These classrooms provide the type of services that is most beneficial for the student's individual learning needs. The lack of distractions, familiar staff, small groups of students, and areas within the room where individual therapies can be performed provide a sense of security for students who need a different but appropriate setting (IDEA, n.d.). Instead of children leaving the classroom for services, most are performed within the room. Therapies such as OT or PT may require the child being moved to a room with specialized equipment.

Individual Therapies and Working with Other Professionals

Parents may choose to retain private therapists to work with their children. In some cases, insurance plans will pay for part of the services, especially if there is a prescription written or services are medically necessary. Many insurance policies will pay for speech and language and physical therapy sessions. When educators recognize, or parents disclose, that a child is receiving outside services, a discussion is warranted, resulting in classroom goals that are aligned with the services. Continuing to use age-appropriate practices and sound curricula will ensure that children will continue to learn (ASHA, 2014).

Society places a stigma on families who are engaged in counseling with social and psychology professionals; conversely, families who recognize the need for services develop an appreciation for positive outcomes often seen from these experiences. Educators who understand the deep commitment families make to secure and persevere through services can become advocates for the family. Positively recognizing families who do so in private enables better relationships to be made that benefit the children in the family (Lifter, Mason, and Barton, 2012).

Wraparound Services

With more parents in the workforce, there is an increased need for both before- and after-school care for their child. Between 11 percent and 27 percent of working parents have the responsibility of finding care for an atypical child (U.S. Dept. of Health and Human Services and U.S. Department of Education, 2015). Finding and securing appropriate care settings with well-educated staff who are knowledgeable about serving children with disabilities can be difficult. Educators can direct families to community programs and can suggest to parents that they use personal recommendations. Many schools offer wraparound care, but it might not necessarily meet the needs of the child. Ensuring that there is a good fit between the family, child, and program will enable the child to find success.

Some school districts write summer or after-school requirements into a child's IEP and provide payment, but most do not, leaving the parents to absorb the cost. Other resources that families can use are bartering care, using community funds or United Way scholarship funds, or altering the work schedule to be home with the child after school or during the summer (Benefit Resources, n.d.). Other solutions include using community-based programs that offer childcare for days when schools are closed or hiring a well-trained person to provide care in the child's home. Caregivers can also be contracted from agencies who train staff to work with children with special needs.

Increasing Communication with Families

Teachers who communicate effectively with families report that problems are easily solved and families participate more in school events and are more comfortable with the instruction, interventions, and therapies their children are receiving (Mead, 2017). Whether old-fashioned handwritten communication notebooks are used or information is conveyed via computer, the method is inconsequential; it is the content that makes the difference.

Short daily notes sent home for children who ride the bus are vital to keeping parents well informed about daily events. Atypical children's families may need more elaborate daily communication that outlines the child's actual day and may contain notes written by individual therapists detailing the services provided for the day and the child's reactions.

Daily phone conferences may be required and more effective for children with severe needs. Some therapists may write daily about the interventions used, whereas the general educator may write less descriptive notes by focusing more on general classroom activities and how the child reacted and participated (Mead, 2017). More and more educators are turning to computer-based programs to communicate with families.

One such free app available on laptops, tablets, and smartphones, is called ClassDoJo. This simple tool allows instant two-way communication, sends pictures or homework snapshots, and translates into the appropriate language for each family (Class Twist, n.d.). Parents should be encouraged to communicate back to educators through the method they feel most comfortable using.

Email and other programs such as Cubbie can be used for written daily communication. It may take time for both educators and families to become comfortable using computer-based programs versus face-to-face conversations. Depending on the languages spoken by the parents of children in the classroom; communication in multiple languages may be necessary.

The Family Educational Rights and Privacy Act (FERPA) (U.S. Department of Education, 2007) mandates how students' records, information communicated with families, disclosure of treatments, and services rendered be maintained and secured. Educators must be careful of the methods they use to disclose information in written or electronic form. General activity-related, non-child-specific information is fine to share with families; however, child-specific activity falls under the FERPA (2007) law.

Any child-specific information shared with parents should be objective and reflect reactions to treatments and therapies, items to work on at home, and questions asked of parents to extend conversation. All written materials can be called by a court of law; therefore, they should be factual and contain no opinions (U.S. Department of Education, 2007). As with any other written incident- or accident-reporting forms, names of other children should be eliminated. Since classroom paraprofessionals often write about general activities in communication books, they need to be trained on the same requirements.

Other methods of communication that are effective are monthly team meetings. Devoid of the formality in which an IEP is developed, these discussions engage all team members and families in communicating about the strategies used across all service areas the child receives. These meetings strive to provide continuity between home and the program, sharing successes and challenges experienced by the families and the program. It is an opportunity to hear from service providers about the most effective strategies that are used in treatments, as well as to quell any fears the parents may have and to hear what the parents find works best at home.

Partaking in Community Resources

Most communities have organizations such as police athletic leagues, Boy and Girl Scouts, and private gyms that offer programming for identified children. These programs provide services for children with like needs. Soccer, gymnastics, and scouting groups provide instructors who have training in working with special needs and who can plan programs that children can benefit from. Many organizations and schools have family and parent support groups that are specific to parents who have identified children (Bayada Home Health Care, 2017). Most educators, special education offices, and parents with other identified students are aware of and willing to share these resources

Parents who take advantage of programs that are dedicated to their child's needs find that there is a wealth of knowledge collectively within such collaborations. Special events planned for families enable them to get to know one another, share stories, and solve difficulties, which result in groups of parents who become active advocates for further services. The outgrowth of services from advocating parents often is more specific to children's needs and serves purposes that only family-driven activities can provide.

FINAL THOUGHTS

Transitions often cause great angst among parents who are unfamiliar with moving from a birth-to-age-three program to more formalized services that are part of a public school (First 5 Shasta, 2012). Educators are frequently the first line of comfort that parents may find who become allies for them with their children. Families may demonstrate feelings of fear and a sense of losing control of the decisions made for their child; instead, it is a time in their child's development when they should feel they have input and impact regarding the services that are given to the student.

Families may find that there are challenges in inclusive programming, including different laws and settings and multiple service providers. IEP meetings have formalized requirements per IDEA, whereas team meetings with service providers, teachers, and parents are a route to understand strategies being used in the classroom and ones that will be effective at home. Team meetings increase communication between parents and the school and set the tone for a positive working relationship. There are many ways in which families and educators can communicate, all of which should be discussed to best suit the family's needs.

Educators who are well equipped in working with atypical children feel that their teacher self-efficacy is paramount (Land, 2017). Educators who lack training with atypical children may sense less self-efficacy; however, professional development and mentorship will improve these skills. Developing the skills necessary to be a proficient teacher goes far in making an inclusive classroom that effectively services the children (Land, 2017).

Mainstream classrooms are a mix of typical and atypical children and may elicit questions from parents. The learning environment looks different, due to the amount of equipment and number of accommodations necessary to fulfill children's needs (Land, 2017). Atypical children are required to spend time in a least restrictive environment or with typical children as role models. Teaching strategies in the classroom may look very different, as some that are used are child specific. Educators who recognize parents' fears can quickly answer questions explaining the purposes of classrooms and interventions used in the room.

Parents who work and have atypical children may require full-time care arrangements. Service providers and educators, as well as community resources, can give referrals for care. Community agencies that work with families often have referral lists and outside programs for children to participate in, such as sports and other activities that support appropriate development. Parents and educators who use effective strategies of communication will find that their relationships will help support their family.

POINTS TO REMEMBER

- *Transitions are difficult for most families when their children move from birth-to-age-three programs to public schools. Educators play an important role in making this transition smooth, understandable, and meaningful for them, which removes the fearfulness families feel.*
- *There are challenges of mainstreaming; educators who have high self-efficacy in their skills maintain and enrich a classroom that is paramount to meeting educational goals of all children.*
- *Laws such as IDEA, ADA, and FERPA need to be followed in all educational settings. It becomes the responsibility of educators and program*

administrators that they are followed throughout the IEP process and in classroom management.

- The special education classroom or learning environment may look different from what families are accustomed to. Educators who are proficient at explaining how it impacts all students will find that families quickly become advocates for all children.
- Families with identified children may need a wide range of community resources, such as wraparound care, recreation opportunities, and services that support the entire family. Knowing community resources and having ways to support bidirectional communication with families is beneficial to supporting the whole child and the child's educational goals.

References

Administration for Children and Families (ACF). (2017a). *History of Head Start*. Retrieved from https://www.acf.hhs.gov/ohs/about/history-of-head-start.
———. (2017b). *Introducing the new Head Start program performance standards*. Retrieved from https://www.acf.hhs.gov/ohs/policy.
———. (2017c). *Policy statement on supporting the development of children who are dual language learners in early childhood programs*. U.S. Department of Health and Human Services. Retrieved from https://www.acf.hhs.gov/sites/default/files/ecd/dll_guidance_document_final.pdf.
Aiger, A. (2017). *Five domains for early childhood development*. Retrieved from http://www.livestrong.com/article/156820-five-domains-for-early-childhood-development/.
Alder, R. B., Rosenfeld, L. B., and Procter, R. (2017). *Interplay: The process of interpersonal communication*. Oxford: Oxford University Press.
Allen, L., and Kelly, B. (2015). *Transforming the workforce for children birth through age 8: A unifying foundation*. Committee on the Science of Children Birth to Age 8: Deepening and Broadening the Foundation for Success; Board on Children, Youth, and Families; Institute of Medicine; National Research Council. Retrieved from https://www.ncbi.nlm.nih.gov/books/NBK310532/pdf/Bookshelf_NBK310532.pdf.
Allyn, P., and Morrell, E. (2016). *Every Child A Super Reader*. Scholastic: New York.
American Academy of Pediatrics, American Public Health Association, National Resource Center for Health and Safety in Child Care and Early Education. (2011). *Caring for our children: National health and safety performance standards; Guidelines for early care and education programs* (3rd ed.). Elk Grove Village, IL: American Academy of Pediatrics; Washington, DC: American Public Health Association. Retrieved from http://nrckids.org.
American Occupational Therapy Association. (2017a). *About occupational therapy: What is Occupational Therapy?* Retrieved from https://www.aota.org/Consumers.aspx.

————. (2017b). *What is occupational therapy: Answering the six Q's—what, who, why, when, where, and how—about occupational therapy.* Retrieved from https://www.aota.org/~/media/Corporate/Files/Practice/Manage/Presentation-Resources/Brochure/What-is-OT-Peds.pdf.

American Physical Therapy Association. (2017). *Physical therapist's guide to developmental delay.* Retrieved from http://www.moveforwardpt.com/symptoms conditionsdetail.aspx?cid=0cb99l6b-6b09-44ab-8708-cfc52eb351f5.

American Psychiatric Association. (2016). *What is specific learning disorder?* Retrieved from https://www.psychiatry.org/patients-families/specific-learning-disorder/what-is-specific-learning-disorder.

American Speech-Language Hearing Association (ASHA). (2014). *Definitions of communication disorders and variations.* Retrieved from https://www.asha.org/policy/RP1993-00208/.

————. (2016). *IDEA Part C: Evaluation and assessment definitions.* Retrieved from https://www.asha.org/Advocacy/federal/idea/IDEA-Part-C-Evaluation-and-Assessment-Definitions/.

Aos, S., Lieb, R., Mayfield, J., Miller, M., and Pennucci, A. (2004). *Benefits and costs of prevention and early intervention programs for youth.* Olympia: Washington State Institute for Public Policy.

Arsaga, A. (2016) *What is chunking?* Parent Cortical Mass. Retrieved from http://www.parentcorticalmass.com/2013/09/what-is-chunking.html.

Association for Psychological Science. (n.d.). *Judy S. DeLoache.* Retrieved from https://www.psychologicalscience.org/publications/observer/25at25/judy-s-deloache.html.

Babcock, E. (2014). *Using brain science to design new pathways out of poverty.* Crittenton Women's Union. Retrieved from http://www.liveworkthrive.org/.

Bann, C. M., Wallander, J. L., Do, B., Thorsten, V., Pasha, O., Biasini, F. J., Belled, R., Goudar, S., Chomba, E., McClure, E., and Carlo, W. S. (2015). Home-based early intervention and the influence of family resources on cognitive development. *Pediatrics, 137*(4). doi: 10.1542/peds.2015-3766.

Barnett, W. S., Carolan, M. E., Squires, J. H., Clarke Brown, K., and Horowitz, M. (2015). *The state of preschool 2014: State preschool yearbook.* New Brunswick, NJ: National Institute for Early Education Research.

Barnett, W. S., and Hustedt, J. T. (2003). Preschool: The most important grade. *Educational Leadership, 60*(7): 54–57. Retrieved from https://eric.ed.gov/?id=EJ666030.

Barnett, W. S., and Masse, L. N. (2007). Early childhood program design and economic returns: Comparative benefit-cost analysis of the Abecedarian program and policy implications. *Economics of Education Review, 26,* 113–25.

Bartik, T. (2014). *From preschool to prosperity: The economic payoff of early childhood education.* Kalamazoo, MI: W.E. Upjohn Institute for Employment Research.

Barton, E. E., and Smith, B. J. (2015). *Preschool inclusion challenges and solutions: A national survey.* Retrieved from http://ectacenter.org/~pdfs/topics/inclusion/inclusion_survey_summary_9.16.pdf.

Bayada Home Health Care. (2017). *Eight support groups for parents raising children with special needs.* Retrieved from http://blog.bayada.com/cares/eight-support-groups-for-parents-raising-children-with-special-needs.

Benasich, A. A., and Choudhury, N. (2012). Timing, information processing, and efficacy: Early factors that impact childhood language trajectories. In A. A. Benasich and R. H. Fitch (Eds.), *Developmental dyslexia: Early precursors, neurobehavioral markers, and biological substrates* (pp. 99–118). Baltimore: Paul H. Brookes Publishing.

Benasich, A., Choudhury, N., Realpe-Bonilla, T., and Roesler, C. (2014). Plasticity in the developing brain: Active auditory exposure impacts prelinguistic acoustic mapping. *The Journal of Neuroscience, 34*(40): 13349–63.

Benasich, A. A., and Fitch, R. H. (2012). *Developmental dyslexia: Early precursors, neurobehavioral markers, and biological substrates.* Baltimore: Paul H. Brookes Publishing.

Benefit Resources. (n.d.). *Child care and development fund.* Retrieved from https://www.benefits.gov/benefits/benefit-details/615.

Berk, L. E. (2017). *Child Development.* Saddle River, N.J.: Pearson Education.

Besharov, D. J., Germanis, P., Higney, C. A., and Call, D. M. (2011). *Currie/Thomas econometric studies: Assessments of twenty-six early childhood evaluations.* School of Public Policy, 1–17. Retrieved from http://www.welfareacademy.org/pubs/early_education/pdfs/Besharov_ECE%20assessments_Currie_Thomas_Econometric%20Studies.pdf.

Bienia, E. J. (2016). *Preschool partnerships: How teachers make sense of their experiences.* (Doctoral dissertation). Northeastern University. Retrieved from ProQuest.

Bierman, K. L., and Motamedi, M. (2015). SEL programs for preschool children. In J. Durlak, C. Domitrovich, R. P. Weissberg, and T. Gullotta (Eds.) *The handbook of social and emotional learning: Research and practice.* New York: Guilford.

Birth Injury Guide. (2017a). *Infant occupational therapy.* Retrieved from http://www.birthinjuryguide.org/birth-injury/treatment/occupational-therapy/.

———. (2017b). *Infant physical therapy.* Retrieved from http://www.birthinjuryguide.org/birth-injury/treatment/physical-therapy/.

———. (2017c). *Speech pathology for infants.* Retrieved from http://www.birthinjuryguide.org/birth-injury/treatment/speech-pathology/.

Bjorklund, D. F., and Causey, K. B. (2018). *Children's thinking: Cognitive development and individual differences.* Los Angeles: Sage.

Blackwell, C.K., Lauricella, A.R., Wartella, E., Robb, M., & Schomberg.R. (2013). *Adoption and use of technology in early education: The interplay of extrinsic barriers and teacher attitudes.* doi: 10.1016/j.compedu.2013.07.024.

Bowlby, J. (1957). An ethological approach to research in child development. *British Journal of Medical Psychology* 30, 230–240. doi: 10.1111/j.2044-8341.1957.tb01202.x.

Bradshaw, W. (2012). A framework for providing culturally responsive early intervention services. *Young Exceptional Children, 16*(1): 3–13. doi: 10.1177/1096250612451757.

Bredikyte, M. (2011). *The zones of proximal development in children's play.* (PhD thesis). University of Oulu, Faculty of Education, Finland. Retrieved from ProQuest.

Brody, A. and Frost, L. (n.d.). *Picture exchange communication system: What is PECS?* Retrieved from https://pecsusa.com/pecs/.

Broekhuizen, M., Slot, P., van Aken, M., and Dubas, J. S. (2016). Teachers' emotional and behavioral support and preschoolers' self-regulation: Relations with social and emotional skills during play. *Early Education and Development, 28*(2): 135–53. doi: 10.10409289.2016.12064458.

Brown, C. P., and Mowry, B. (2015). *Closing early learning gaps with rigorous DAP.* doi: 10.1177/0031721715579041.

Brumariu, L. E. (2015). Parent–child attachment and emotion regulation. In G. Bosmans and K. A. Kerns (Eds.), "Attachment in middle childhood: Theoretical advances and new directions in an emerging field." *New Directions for Child and Adolescent Development,* 148, 31–45.

Camilli, G., Vargas, S., Ryan, S., and Barnett, W. S. (2010). Meta-Analysis of the effects of early education interventions on cognitive and social development. *Teachers College Record, 112*(3): Article 15440. Retrieved from http://www.gregorycamilli.info/papers/early%20education%20interventions.pdf.

Campbell, F. A. (2014). *High quality early education and care bring health benefits 30 years later.* Retrieved from http://fpg.unc.edu/news/high-quality-early-education-and-care-bring-health-benefits-30-years-later.

Cancialosi, C. (2014). *6 keys to influencing effective knowledge transfer in your business.* Retrieved from https://www.forbes.com/sites/chriscancialosi/2014/12/08/6-key-steps-to-influencing-effective-knowledge-transfer-in-your-business/3/#2508b7072654.

Carlo, M., Barr, C., August, D., Calderon, M., and Artzi, L. (2014). Language of instruction as moderator for transfer of reading comprehension skills among Spanish-speaking English language learners. *Bilingual Research Journal, 37*(3): 287–310.

Carlson, S., Lelazo, P. D., and Faja, S. (2013). *The Oxford handbook of developmental psychology.* doi:10.1093/oxfordhb/9780199958450.013.0025.

Center for Parent Information and Resources. (2012). *Parent notification and consent.* Retrieved from http://www.parentcenterhub.org/ei-notification-consent/.

———. (2014). *Overview of Early Intervention.* Retrieved from http://www.parentcenterhub.org/ei-overview/#eval.

———. (2016). *Writing the IFSP for your child.* Retrieved from http://www.parentcenterhub.org/ifsp/.

Center for Parenting Education. (2017). *What is persistence?* Retrieved from http://centerforparentingeducation.org/library-of-articles/child-development/understanding-temperament-persistence/.

Centers for Disease Control (CDC). (2014). *Families with special needs: Caregivers tips.* Retrieved from https://www.cdc.gov/family/specialneeds/index.htm.

———. (2015). *Developmental disabilities.* Retrieved from https://www.cdc.gov/ncbddd/developmentaldisabilities/about.html.

Cheathum, G. A., and Ostrosky, M. M. (2009). Listening for details of talk: Early childhood parent-teacher conference communication facilitators. *Young Exceptional Children, 13*(1): 36–49. doi: 10.1177/1096250609347283.

Chen, F., and Fleer, M. (2016) A cultural-historical reading of how play is used in families as a tool for supporting children's emotional development in everyday life. *European Early Childhood Education Research Journal, 24*(2): 305–19.

Class Twist. (n.d.). *ClassDojo connects teachers with students and parents to build amazing classroom communities.* Retrieved from https://www.classdojo.com/#LearnMore.

Community Products, LLC. (2017). *Rifton chairs.* Retrieved from https://www.rifton.com/products/special-needs-chairs/rifton-activity-chairs.

Connecticut Early Learning and Development Standards (CT ELDS). (2014). *Connecticut early learning development guidelines.* Retrieved from http://www.sde.ct.gov/sde/lib/sde/pdf/backtoschool/ctelds_whatchildren_birthtofive_should_know_and_be_able_to_do.pdf.

———. (2015). *Connecticut early learning guidelines for diverse learners.* Retrieved from http://www.ct.gov/oec/lib/oec/DiverseLearnersApril_26_2016_Finalw.pdf.

Core Knowledge Foundation. (2013). *Unit 2: Assessment and Remediation Guide: Skills Strand: Kindergarten.* Retrieved from https://www.engageny.org/sites/default/files/downloadable-resources/ckla_gk_arg_unit2_engage.pdf.

Council for Accreditation of Educator Preparation (CAEP). (2013). *2013 CAEP Standards.* Retrieved from http://caepnet.org/~/media/Files/caep/standards/caep-standards-one-pager-061716.pdf?la=en.

Council for Exceptional Children. (2017). *DEC recommended practices for early intervention.* Missoula, MT: DEC.

Cox-Peterson, A. (2011). *Educational partnership: Connecting schools, families, and the community.* Thousand Oaks, CA: Sage Publications.

Crisalli, L. (2016). Inclusiveness in action. *Exchange, 38*(4): 46–49. Retrieved from https://dcf.wisconsin.gov/files/ccic/pdf/articles/inclusiveness-in-action.pdf.

Daugherty, L., Dossani, R., John, E., and Wright, C. (2014). *Families, powered on: Improving family engagement in early childhood through technology.* Retrieved from https://www.rand.org/content/dam/rand/pubs/research_reports/RR600/RR673z5/RAND_RR673z5.pdf.

David, L. (2014). Social development theory (Vygotsky). Learning Theories. Retrieved from https://www.learning-theories.com/vygotskys-social-learning-theory.html.

Davidson, R. J., and McEwen, B. S. (2012). Social influences on neuroplasticity: Stress and interventions to promote well-being. *Nature Neuroscience, 15*(5): 689–95.

Davis-Temple, J., Jung, S., and Sainato, D. (2014). Teaching young children with special needs and their peers to play board games: Effects of a least to most prompting procedure to increase independent performance. *Behavioral Analyst in Practice, 7*(1): 21–30. doi: 10.1007/s40617-014-0001-8.

DeBord, K. (2016). U.S. cooperative extension parent educator's framework. In J. J. Ponzetti Jr. (Ed.), *Evidence-based parenting education: A global perspective.* New York: Routledge.

Decker, C. L. (2016). *ESEA, disability and the lessons of the past.* Retrieved from https://www.huffingtonpost.com/curtis-l-decker-jd/esea-disability-and-the-l_b_8155228.html.

Diamond, A., and Lee, K. (2011) Interventions shown to aid executive function development in children 4 to 12 years old. *Science, 333*, August 19, 959–64.

Diehl, D., and Mcfarland, D. A. (2012). Classroom ordering and the situational imperatives of routine and ritual. *Sociology of Education, 85,* 326–49. doi:10.1177/0038040712452093.

Doar, R., and Wassink, B. (2015). *America's broken program for low-income children with disabilities—and what to do about it.* Retrieved from http://www.aei.org/publication/americas-broken-program-low-income-children-disabilities/.

Dombro, A. L., Jablon, J. R., and Stetson, C. (2011). *Powerful interactions: How to connect with children to extend their learning.* Maine: Stenhouse.

Dominica, S. (2015). Creating the right environment for inclusion classrooms. Retrieved from http://www.brighthubeducation.com/special-ed-inclusion-strategies/68102-creating-the-right-environment-in-your-inclusive-classroom/.

Drang, D. (2011). *Preschool teachers' beliefs, knowledge, and practices related to classroom management.* (Doctoral dissertation). University of Maryland. Retrieved from ProQuest.

Duncan, A. (2014). *Department of Education release of new family engagement framework.* Retrieved from https://www.youtube.com/watch?v=BR2e0HVKa4U.

———. (2015). ESEA speech to Congress. Retrieved from https://www.ed.gov/news/speeches/remarks-us-secretary-education-arne-duncan-50th-anniversary-congress-passing-elementary-and-secondary-education-act.

Dunst, C. J., Trivette, C. M., Hamby, D. W., and Simkus, A. (2013). Systematic review of studies promoting the use of assistive technology devices by young children with disabilities. *Tots N Tech Research Brief, 8*(1): 1–21. Retrieved from https://eric.ed.gov/?id=ED565254.

Durand, T. (2011). Latina mothers' cultural beliefs about their children, parent roles and education: Implications for effective and empowering home-school partnerships. *Urban Review.* doi:10.1007/s11256-010-0167-5.

Eichenstein, R. (2015). *Not what I expected: Help and hope for parents of atypical children.* New York: Penguin Books.

Epstein, J. L. (1987). Toward a theory of family-school connections: Teacher practices and parent involvement across the school years. In K. Hurrelmann, F. Kaufmann, and F. Losel (Eds.), *Social Intervention: Potential and constraints* (pp. 121–36). New York: de Gruyter.

Epstein, J. L. (1995). School, family, community partnerships: Caring for the children we share. *Phi Delta Kappan, 76*(9): 701–12.

Epstein, J. L. (2011). *School, family, and community partnerships: Preparing educators and improving schools* (2nd ed.). Boulder, CO: Westview Press.

Epstein, J. L., Sanders, M. G., Simon, B. S., Salinas, K. C., Jansorn, N. R., and Van Voorhis, F. L. (2002). *School, family, and community partnerships: Your handbook for action* (2nd ed.). Thousand Oaks, CA: Corwin.

Equestrian Therapy. (2017). *Equestrian therapy for children with disability.* Retrieved from http://www.equestriantherapy.com/equestrian-therapy-disabled-children/.

Escueta, M., Whetten, K., Ostermann, J., and O'Donnell, K. (2014). Adverse childhood experiences, psychosocial well-being and cognitive development among orphans and abandoned children in five low income countries. *BMC International Health and Human Rights, 14*(6). doi: 10.1186/1472-698X-14-6.

Evans, B. (2016). *Making transitions from home to school easy.* Retrieved from https://secure.highscope.org/img/product/description/BirthdayPartyReproducible pages.pdf.

Executive Office of the President of the United States. (2015). *The economics of early childhood investment.* Retrieved from https://obamawhitehouse.archives.gov/sites/ default/files/docs/early_childhood_report_update_final_non-embargo.pdf.

Ferholt, B., and Rainio, A. P. (2016). Teacher support of student engagement in early childhood: Embracing ambivalence through playworlds. *Early Years.* Retrieved from https://www.researchgate.net/profile/Anna_Rainio/publication/ 294105656_Teacher_support_of_student_engagement_in_early_childhood_ embracing_ambivalence_through_playworlds/links/570e145208ae319988 9cf319/.

Ferlazzo, L. (2011). Involvement or engagement? *Education Leadership.* Retrieved from https://eric.ed.gov/?id=EJ932180.

Ferrer, E., Shaywitz, B., Holahan, J., Marchione, K., Michaels, R., and Shaywitz, S. (2015). Achievement gap in reading is present as early as first grade and persists through adolescence. *Journal of Pediatrics, 167,* 1121–25.

Fielding, L., Kerr, N., and Rosier, P. (2007). *Annual growth for all students, catch-up growth for those who are behind.* Kennewick, WA: New Foundations Press.

Filippello, P., Marino, F., Spadaro, L., and Sorrenti, L. (2013). Learning disabilities and social problem solving skills. *Mediterranean Journal of Clinical Psychology, 1*(2). doi: 10.6092/2282-1619/2013.2.911.

First 5 Shasta. (2012). *Countdown to kindergarten for the child with special needs: An informational guide for parents and primary caregivers.* Retrieved from https:// www.shastacoe.org/uploaded/Dept/selpa/CAC/Countdown_to_Kindergarten_ Final_Eng.pdf.

First Five Years Fund. (2016). *Our Mission.* Retrieved from https://ffyf.org/.

FitzGerald, M. A. (2011), Engaging Latino parents in the middle: Valuing, validating, and building upon what families already do. In Ian E. Sutherland, Karen L. Sanzo, Jay Paredes Scribner (Eds.), Leading small and mid-sized urban school districts. *Advances in Educational Administration, 22,* 129–54.

Flamboyan Classroom Family Engagement Rubric (2011). Flamboyan Institute. Washington, DC, and Puerto Rico. Retrieved from http://www.roadmapproject .org/wp-content/uploads/2012/11/Final-Report_Engaged-Parents-Successful- Students-Report-9-12-12.pdf.

Fleer, M. (2015). Pedagogical positioning in play—teachers being inside and outside of children's imaginary play. *Early Childhood Development, 185*(11–12): 1801–14.

Fleming, S. (2015). *Checklist of early childhood developmental skills.* Retrieved from http://www.livestrong.com/article/520636-checklist-of-early-childhood-developmental-skills/.

Follari, L. (2015). *Foundations and best practices in early childhood education: History, Theories, and approaches to learning* (3rd ed.). New York: Pearson.

Foundations Developmental House. (2017). *Motor and oral motor milestones for feeding development.* Retrieved from https://www.fdhkids.com/developmental_milestones/feeding_development.html.

Froesen, A., Hanson, M., and Martin, K. (2015). In the eyes of the beholder: Cultural considerations in interpreting children's behavior. *Young Exceptional Children, 18*(4). doi:10.1177/1096250614535222.

Galinsky, E. (2010). *Mind in the making.* New York: HarperCollins.

Gestwicki, C. (2017). *Developmentally appropriate practice.* Boston: Cengage.

Gibson, S., and Dembo, M. H. (1984). Teacher efficacy: A construct validation. *Journal of Educational Psychology, 76*(4): 569–82.

Gillanders. C., McKinney, M., and Ritchie, S. (2012). What kind of school would you like for your children? Exploring minority mothers' beliefs to promote home-school partnerships. *Early Childhood Education, 40*, 285–94. doi: 10.1007/s10643-012-0514-0.

Gilliam, W. S., and Zigler, E. F. (2001). A critical meta-analysis of all evaluations of state-funded preschools from 1977 to 1998: Implications for policy, service delivery and program evaluation. *Early Childhood Research Quarterly, 15*(4): 441–73.

Glennen, S. (2014). Internationally adopted children in the early school years: Relative strengths and weaknesses in language abilities. *Language, Speech, and Hearing Services in Schools, 46,* 1–13. doi: 10.1044/2014_LSHSS-13-0042.

Gormley, W., Philips, D., and Gayer, T. (2008). The early years: Preschool programs can boost school readiness. *Science, 320,* 1723–24.

Grant, K. B., and Ray, J. A. (2016). *Home, school, and community collaboration: Culturally responsive family engagement* (3rd ed.). Thousand Oaks, CA: Sage Publications.

Grigorenko, E. (2012). What educators should know about the state of research on genetic influences on reading and reading disability. In A. A. Benasich and R. H. Fitch (Eds.), *Developmental dyslexia: Early precursors, neurobehavioral markers, and biological substrates* (pp. 62–78). Baltimore: Paul H. Brookes Publishing.

Hakkarainen, P., Bredikyte, M., Jakkula, K., and Munter, H. (2013). Adult play guidance and children's play development in a narrative play-world. *European Early Childhood Education Research Journal, 21*(2): 213–25.

Hamilton-Jones, B. M., and Vail, C. O. (2014). Preparing special educators for collaboration in the classroom: Pre-service teachers' beliefs and perspectives. *International Journal of Special Education, 29*(1): 56–86. Retrieved from http://files.eric.ed.gov/fulltext/EJ1013700.pdf.

Hammer, C. S., Hoff, E., Uchikoshi, Y., Gillanders, C., Castro, D., and Sandilos, L. (2014). The language and literacy development of young dual language learners: A critical review. *Early Child Research Quarterly, 29*(4): 715–33. doi: 10.1016/j.ecresq.2014.05.008.

Han, Y. C. (2012). From survivor to leaders: Stages of immigrant family involvement. *Innovative Voices in Education: Engaging Diverse Communities.* Retrieved from www.innovativevoicesineducation.com.

Hanson, J. L., Hair, N., Shen, D. G., Shi, F., Gilmore, J. H., Wolfe, B. L., and Pollack, S. D. (2013). *Family poverty affects the rate of human infant brain growth.* doi: 10.1371/journal.pone.0080954.

Harlow, H. F. (1958). The nature of love. *American Psychologist* 13, 673–685. doi: 10.1037/h0047884.

Harris, S. L., and Bruey, C. T. (2016). Families of the developmentally disabled. In I. R. H. Falloon (Ed.), *Handbook of Behavioural Family Therapy* (pp.181–202). New York: Routledge.

Harvard Family Research Project. (2014). *Redefining family engagement for student success.* Retrieved from http://www.hfrp.org/redefining-family-engagement-for-student-success.

Haynes, J. (n.d.). Stages of second language acquisition. *Everything ESL.* Retrieved from http://www.everythingesl.net/inservices/language_stages.php.

Healy, J. M. (1999). *Endangered minds: Why children don't think and what we can do about it.* New York: Touchstone.

Hebbeler, K., and Spiker, D. (2016). Supporting young children with disabilities. *The Future of Children, 26*(2): 185–205. Retrieved from https://eric .ed.gov/?id=EJ1118562.

Heckman, J. J., Moon, S. H., Pinto, R., Savelyev, P., and Yavitz, A. (2010). NBER Working Paper 16180.2010. *A new cost-benefit and rate of return analysis for the Perry Preschool Program: A summary.* Retrieved from http://ftp.iza.org/ pp17.pdf.

Heer, K., Rose, J., and Larkin, M. (2016). The challenges of providing culturally competent care within a disability focused team: A phenomenological exploration of staff experiences. *Journal of Transcultural Nursing, 27*(2): 109–16. doi:10.1177/1043659614526454.

Henniger, M. L. (2013). *Teaching young children.* Saddle River, NJ: Pearson.

Hernandez, J. (2012). *Double jeopardy: How third-grade reading skills and poverty influence high school graduation.* Baltimore: Annie E. Casey Foundation.

HighScope. (2017). *Let's explore potential together.* Retrieved from https://highscope .org/curriculum.

Hirsch, B. (2016). *Cooperative group play social skills training for children with social, emotional, and behavior challenges: Impact on self-esteem and social skills.* PCOM Psychology Dissertations, Paper 374.

Hoff, E. (2013). Interpreting the early language trajectories of children from low-SES and language minority homes: Implications for closing achievement gaps. *Developmental Psychology, 49*(1): 4–14. Retrieved from https://www.ncbi.nlm.nih.gov/ pubmed/22329382.

Hoff, E., and Tian, C. (2005). Socioeconomic status and cultural influences on language. *Journal of Communication Disorders, 38*, 271–78.

Hoy, W. K., and Woolfork, A. E. (1993). Teachers' sense of efficiency and the organizational health of schools. *The Elementary School Journal, 93*, 356–72.

Humphries, J., and Rains, K. (2017). *A fighting chance: Supporting young children experiencing disruptive change.* St. Paul, MN: Redleaf.

Hynes, W. (2014). Meet the family. *Teaching Tolerance,* 48–50. Retrieved from https://www.tolerance.org/magazine/fall-2014/meet-the-family.

Individuals with Disabilities Act (IDEA). (n.d.). Retrieved from https://sites.ed.gov/idea/.

Isaacs, J. B. (2012). *Starting school at a disadvantage: The school readiness of poor children.* Retrieved from https://www.brookings.edu/wp-content/uploads/2016/06/0319_school_disadvantage_isaacs.pdf.

Jamison, K. E., Forston, L. D., and Stanton-Chapman, T. L. (2012). Encouraging social skill development through play in early childhood special education classes. *Young Exceptional Children, 15*(2): 3–19. Retrieved from http://www.mdpi.com/2227-9067/1/1/5/htm.

Jasis, P. M., and Ordoñez-Jasis, R. (2012). Latino parent involvement: Examining commitment and empowerment in schools. *Urban Education, 47,* 65–89.

Jiang, Y., Ekono, M., and Skinner, C. (2014). Basic facts about low-income children: Children under 6 years, 2012. National Center for Children in Poverty, Columbia University Mailman School of Public Health. Retrieved from http://www.nccp.org/publications/pdf/text_1088.pdf.

Johnson, F. (2015). A school for children and their parents. *The Atlantic.* Retrieved from https://www.theatlantic.com/education/archive/2015/01/a-school-for-childrenand-their-parents/384333/.

Jung, S. and Sainato, D. M. (2013). Teaching play skills to young children with autism. *Journal of Intellectual & Developmental Disability, 38,* 74–90. doi: 10.3109/13668250.2012.732220.

K12 Academics. (2017). *History of preschool in the United States.* Retrieved from http://www.k12academics.com/systems-formal-education/preschool-education/history-preschool-united-states.

Kennedy, J. F. (n.d.). Quote. Retrieved from https://www.brainyquote.com/quotes/quotes/j/johnfkenn131489.html.

Klein, A. (2016). *The Every Student Succeeds Act: An ESSA overview.* Retrieved from http://www.edweek.org/ew/issues/every-student-succeeds-act/index.html.

Knoche, L. L., Marvin, C. A., and Sheridan, S. M. (2014). *Parent engagement during home visits in early Head Start and Head Start: Useful strategies for practitioners.* Retrieved from https://journals.uncc.edu/dialog/article/viewFile/423/413.

Konishi, H., Kanero, J., Freeman, M. R., Michnick-Golinkoff, R., and Hirsh-Pasek, K. (2014). Six principals of language development: Implications for second language learners. *Developmental Neuropsychology, 39*(5). doi: 10.1080/87565641.2014.931961.

Krakower, B., and Plante, S. L. (2016). *Using technology to engage students with learning disabilities.* Thousand Oaks, CA: Corwin.

Kraus, L. (2017). *2016 disability statistics annual report.* Durham: University of New Hampshire. Retrieved from https://disabilitycompendium.org/sites/default/files/user-uploads/2016_AnnualReport.pdf.

Kummerer, S. E. (2010). Language intervention for Hispanic children with language-learning disabilities: evidence based practice. *Intervention in School and Clinic, 45*(3): 192–200. Retrieved from https://eric.ed.gov/?id=EJ874394.

Lamy, C., Barnett, W. S., and Jung, K. (2006). *The effects of Oklahoma's early childhood four-year-old program on young children's school readiness.* Retrieved from http://nieer.org/wp-content/uploads/2005/12/ok.pdf.

Land, S. (2017). *Effective teaching practices for students in inclusive classrooms.* Retrieved from http://education.wm.edu/centers/ttac/resources/articles/inclusion/effectiveteach/.

Leffel, K., and Suskind, D. (2013). Parent-directed approaches to enrich the early language environments of children living in poverty. *Seminars in Speech and Language, 34*(4): 194–204. doi: 10.1055/s-0033-1353443.

Lifter, K., Mason, E. J., and Barton, E. E. (2012). Children's play: Where we have been and where we could go. *Journal of Early Intervention, 33*, 281–97. doi: 10.1177/1053815111429465.

Li-Grining, C. P. (2007). Effortful control among low-income preschoolers in three cities: Stability, change, and individual differences. *Developmental Psychology, 43*(1): 208–21. doi: 10.1037/0012-1649.43.1.208.

Lillard, A. S., Lerner, M. D., Hopkins, E. J., Dore, R. A., Smith, E. D., and Palmquist, C. M. (2013). The impact of pretend play on children's development: A review of the evidence. *Psychological Bulletin, 139*(1): 1–34. Retrieved from https://pdfs.semanticscholar.org/d20a/da9e8ae8ce3e873d5b885bb4342efebb7788.pdf.

Losardo, A., and Notari Syverson, A. (2011). *Alternative approaches to assessing young children* (2nd ed.). Baltimore: Paul H. Brookes Publishing.

LoTurco, J., Tarkar, A., and Yue Che, A. (2012). Loss of the dyslexia susceptibility gene DCDC2 increases synaptic connectivity in the mouse neocortex. In A. A. Benasich and R. H. Fitch (Eds.), *Developmental dyslexia: Early precursors, neurobehavioral markers, and biological substrates* (pp. 16–31). Baltimore: Paul H. Brookes Publishing.

Lupattelli, A., Picinardi, M., Einarson, A., and Nordeng, H. (2014). Health literacy and its association with perception of teratogenic risks and health behavior during pregnancy. *Patient Education and Counseling.* Retrieved from http://dx.doi.org/10.1016/j.pec.2014.04.014.

Lynch, R., and Vaghul, K. (2015). *The benefits and costs of investing in early childhood education: The fiscal, economic, and societal gains of a universal prekindergarten program in the United States, 2016–2050.* Retrieved from http://cdn.equitablegrowth.org/wp-content/uploads/2015/12/02110123/early-childhood-ed-report-web.pdf.

Maassen, B., van der Leij, A., Maurits, N., and Zwarts, F. (2012). Neurolinguistic and neurophysiological precursors of dyslexia: Selective studies from the Dutch dyslexia programme. In A. A. Benasich and R. H. Fitch (Eds.), *Developmental dyslexia: Early precursors, neurobehavioral markers, and biological substrates* (pp. 119–32). Baltimore: Paul H. Brookes Publishing.

Mapp, K. (2014). *Family engagement as a systemic sustained, and integrated strategy to promote student achievement.* Harvard Family Research Project.

Mapp, K. L., and Kuttner, P. J. (2013). *Partners in education: A dual capacity-building framework for family-school partnerships.* Retrieved from http://www.ed.gov/parent-and-family-engagement.

Marino, C., Mascheretti, S., Facoetti, A., and Molteni, M. (2012). Investigations of candidate genes in families with dyslexia. In A. A. Benasich and R. H. Fitch (Eds.), *Developmental dyslexia: Early precursors, neurobehavioral markers, and biological substrates* (pp. 46–61). Baltimore: Paul H. Brookes Publishing.

Masur, E. F., Flynn, V., and Olson, J. (2015). The presence of background television during young children's play in American homes. *Journal of Children and Media, 9*(3). doi: 10.1080/17482798.2015.1056818.

Mead, A. E. (2017). *Understanding parents' school experiences and how it influences their intent to engage with their child's school* (Unpublished doctoral dissertation). Northeastern University, Boston.

Merriam-Webster. (2017). *Dictionary.* Retrieved from https://www.merriam-webster.com/.

Merrill, S. (2015). *Head start and the evolving concept of family involvement.* Head Start. Retrieved from https://drupaldemo1.cleverex.com/archive/about-us/article/head-start-evolving-concept-family-involvement.

Merritt, E. G., Wanless, S. B., Rimm-Kaufman, S. E., and Peugh, J. L. (2012). The contribution of teachers' emotional support to children's social behaviors and self-regulatory skills in first grade. *School Psychology Review, 41*(2): 141–59.

Meyers, J. A., Mann, M. B., and Becker, J. (2011). The five-year follow-up: Teachers' perceptions of the benefits of home visits for early elementary children. *Early Childhood Education Journal, 39*(3): 191–96. doi: 10.1007/s10643-011-0461-1.

Michael-Luna, S. (2015). What parents have to teach us about their dual language children. *Young Child, 70*(5): 42043. Retrieved from https://drupaldemo1.cleverex.com/archive/about-us/article/head-start-evolving-concept-family-involvement.

Michel, S. (2011). *The history of child care in the U.S. social welfare history project.* Retrieved from http://socialwelfare.library.vcu.edu/programs/child-care-the-american-history/.

Miller, P. H. (2016). *Theories of developmental psychology* (6th ed.). Madison, NY: Worth Publishers.

Morena, M. A. (2016). Supporting child play. *JAMA Pediatrics Parents Page, 170*(2). doi: 10.1001/jamapediatrics.2015.2505.

Myer, G. D., Faigenbaum, A. D., Edwards, N. M., Clark, J. F., Best, T. M., and Sallis, R. E. (2015). Sixty minutes of what? A developing brain perspective for activating children with an integrative exercise approach. *British Journal of Special Medicine, 49*(23): 1510–16. doi: 10.1136/bjsports-2014-093661.

National Association for the Education of Young Children (NAEYC). (n.d.). *About NAEYC.* Retrieved from http://www.naeyc.org/content/about-naeyc.

National Association for the Education of Young Children (NAEYC). (2009a). *Key Messages of the position statement.* Retrieved from http://www.naeyc.org/files/naeyc/file/positions/KeyMessages.pdf.

————. (2009b). *Where we stand: On curriculum, assessment, and program evaluation.* Retrieved from http://www.naeyc.org/files/naeyc/file/positions/Stand CurrAss.pdf.

————. (2009c). *Where we stand: On early learning standards.* Retrieved from http://www.naeyc.org/files/naeyc/file/positions/earlyLearningStandards.pdf.

————. (2009d). *Where we stand: On assessing English language learners.* Retrieved from http://www.naeyc.org/files/naeyc/file/positions/WWSEnglish LanguageLearnersWeb.pdf.

————. (2009e). *Where we stand: Professional preparation standards.* Retrieved from http://www.naeyc.org/files/naeyc/file/positions/programStandards.pdf.

————. (2012). *Technology and interactive media as tools in early childhood programs serving children from birth through age 8.* Retrieved from https://www .naeyc.org/sites/default/files/globally-shared/downloads/PDFs/resources/topics/ PS_technology_WEB.pdf.

————. (2016). *The 10 NAEYC program standards.* Retrieved from https://families .naeyc.org/accredited-article/10-naeyc-program-standards.

National Center for Learning Disabilities. (2014). *The state of learning disabilities* (3rd ed.). Retrieved from http://www.ncld.org/wp-content/uploads/2014/11/2014- State-of-LD.pdf.

National Center on Early Childhood Quality Assurance. (n.d.). Early childhood training and technical assistance system. Retrieved from https://childcareta.acf.hhs.gov/ centers/national-center-early-childhood-quality-assurance.

National Education Association. (2013). *Unions, districts and communities to the table in the NEA Foundation closing the achievement gaps initiative sites.* NEA Foundation Issue Brief Number 7. Retrieved from https://feaweb.org/_data/ files/2013_Generic_PDFs/LeeCountycommunity-engagement-issuebrief.pdf0.pdf.

National Research Council. (2001). *Eager to learn: Educating our preschoolers.* Washington, DC: National Academy Press.

National Scientific Council on the Developing Child (2007). *The timing and quality of early experiences combine to shape brain architecture: Working paper 5.* http:// www.developingchild.net.

————. (2010a). *Early experiences can alter gene expression and affect long-term development: Working paper 10.* http://www.developingchild.net.

————. (2010b). *Persistent fear and anxiety can affect young children's learning and development: Working paper 9.* http://www.developingchild.net.

————. (2011). *Building the brain's "air traffic control" system: How early experiences shape the development of executive function: Working paper 11.* http://www .developingchild.net.

————. (2012). *Establishing a level foundation for life: Mental health begins in early childhood: Working paper 6* (Updated ed.). http://www.developingchild.harvard .edu.

————. (2014). *Excessive stress disrupts the architecture of the developing brain: Working paper 3.* (Updated ed.). http://www.developingchild.harvard.edu.

No Child Left Behind (NCLB). (2002). *Parental involvement: Title I.* Washington, DC: U.S. Department of Education. Retrieved from www2.ed.gov/nclb/landing .jhtml.

Northwestern University. (2014). Parenting in the age of digital technology: A national survey. Retrieved from http://cmhd.northwestern.edu/wp-content/uploads/2015/06/ParentingAgeDigitalTechnology.REVISED.FINAL_.2014.pdf.

Office of the Education Ombudsman. (2012). *Washington state road map project.* Retrieved from http://www.roadmapproject.org/resources/useful-links/.

Opp, A. (2017). *Occupational therapy in early intervention: Helping children succeed.* Retrieved from https://www.aota.org/About-Occupational-Therapy/Professionals/CY/Articles/Early-Intervention.aspx.

Palmer, J. (2016). *Tulsa Head Start program produces lasting positive effects.* Retrieved from http://kgou.org/post/study-tulsa-head-start-program-produces-lasting-positive-effects.

Parents as Teachers (PAT). (2017). *We're going to school: A parent involvement approach to school transitions.* Retrieved from https://static1.squarespace.com/static/56be46a6b6aa60dbb45e41a5/t/57eac0fcc534a59d49fec2f6/1475002621136/Fact-Sheet_SchoolTransitions_10_2_12.pdf.

Parent Teacher Home Visits. (2016). *PTHV Model.* Retrieved from http://www.pthvp.org/what-we-do/pthv-model/.

Park, M. H., Dimitrov, D. M., Das, A., and Gichuru, M. (2014). The teacher efficacy for inclusive practices (TEIP) scale: dimensionality and factor structure. *Journal of Research in Special Educational Needs, 16*(1): 2–12. doi: 10.1111/1471-3802.12047.

Patino, A. (2017). *What you need to know about speech therapy.* Retrieved from https://www.understood.org/en/learning-attention-issues/treatments-approaches/therapies/what-you-need-to-know-about-speech-therapy.

Peak, C. (2015). *The life-changing program Head Start turns 50: A conversation with its founder.* Retrieved from http://nationswell.com/head-start-edward-zigler-founding-of-program/.

Pem, D. (2015). Factors affecting early childhood growth and development: Golden 1000 days. *Adv Practice Nursing.* doi: 10.4172/2573-0347.1000101.

Peterson, A. (n.d.). *Get a grip: Developing fine motor skills in children.* Retrieved from https://familyshare.com/3469/get-a-grip-developing-fine-motor-skills-in-children.

Phillips, D. A., Crowell, N. A., Sussman, A. L., Gunnar, M., Fox, N., Hane, A. A., and Bisgaier, J. (2012). Reactive temperament and sensitivity to context in childcare. *Social Development, 21*(3): 628–43. doi: 10.1111/j.1467-9507.2011.00649.x.

Phillips, S. (2017). *Developing teacher capacity with culturally responsive classroom management practices.* Retrieved from https://pilotscholars.up.edu/cgi/viewcontent.cgi?article=1039&context=etd.

Piaget, J. (1936). *Origins of intelligence in the child.* London: Routledge.

Podvey, M. C., Hinojosa, J., and Koenig, K. P. (2013). Reconsidering insider status for families during the transition from early intervention to preschool special education. *The Journal of Special Education, 46*(4): 211–22. doi: 10.1177/0022466911407074.

Powers, J. (2016). *Parent engagement in early learning.* St. Paul, MN: Red Leaf Press.

Prado, E. L., and Dewey, K. G. (2014). Nutrition and brain development in early life. *Nutrition Review, 72*(4): 267–84. Retrieved from https://academic.oup.com/nutritionreviews/article/72/4/267/1859597.

President and Fellows at Harvard College. (2017). *Executive function & self-regulation.* Center on the Developing Child. Retrieved from https://developingchild.harvard.edu/science/key-concepts/executive-function/.

Psychology Today. (2017). Understanding cognition. Retrieved from https://www.psychologytoday.com/basics/cognition.

Raffinews. (2017). *Children's music.* Retrieved from http://www.raffinews.com/store/childrens-music#.WfFJ6GiPJPY.

Raty, H. (2010). Do parents' own memories contribute to their satisfaction with their child's school? *Educational Studies, 36*(5): 581–84. doi: 10/1080/03055691003729005.

Reed, P. (2017). *Getting started with assistive technology.* Retrieved from http://www.mychildwithoutlimits.org/plan/assistive-technology/getting-started-with-assistive-technology/.

Reynolds, A., Temple, J., Robertson, D., and Mann, E. (2001). Long-term benefits of early intervention on education and crime. *Journal of the American Medical Association, 285*(18): 2339–46.

Rogers-Sirin, L., Ryce, P., and Sirin, S. R. (2014). Acculturation, acculturative stress, and cultural mismatch and their influences on immigrant children and adolescents' wellbeing. In R. Dimitrova, M. Bender, and F. Van de Vijver (Eds.), *Global perspectives on wellbeing in Immigrant families* (pp. 11–30). New York: Springer Science + Business Media.

Rosenberg, S. A., Robinson, C. C., Shaw, E. F., and Ellison, M. C. (2013). *Part C early intervention for infants and toddlers: Percentage eligible versus served.* Retrieved from http://pediatrics.aappublications.org/content/131/1/38.

Rosin, H. (2013). The touch screen generation. *The Atlantic.* Retrieved from http://www.theatlantic.com/magazine/archive/2013/04/the-touch-screen-generation/309250/.

Sanchez, C. (2016). *We learned a lot about how preschool can help kids.* Retrieved from http://www.npr.org/sections/ed/2016/12/27/504712171/we-learned-a-lot-in-2016-about-how-preschool-can-help-kids.

Schuengel, C., de Schipper, J. C., Sterkenburg, P. S., and Kef, S. (2013). Attachment, intellectual disabilities and mental health: Research, assessment and intervention. *Journal of Applied Resources in Intellectual Disabilities, 26,* 34–46. doi: 10.1111/jar.12010.

Schweinhart, L. J., Montie, J., Xiang, Z., Barnett, W. S., Belfield, C. R., and Nores, M. (2005). *Lifetime effects: The High/Scope Perry Preschool Study through Age 40: Summary, conclusions, and frequently asked questions.* Retrieved from http://www.highscope.org/file/Research/PerryProject/specialsummary_rev2011_02_2.pdf.

SELD. (2013). *Robust partnerships that boost student learning.* Retrieved from http://www.sedl.org/about/successstory/20100101_284.html.

Sharma, V., Loreman, T., and Forlin, C. (2012). Measuring teacher efficacy to implement inclusive practices. *Journal of Research in Special Education Needs, 2*(1): 12–21. doi/10.1111/j.1471-3802.2011.01200.x/full.

Shenfield, T, (2015). Teaching social skills to children with Asperger's. *Advanced Psychology.* Retrieved from https://www.psy-ed.com/wpblog/teaching-social-skills-to-children-with-aspergers/.

Singer, E., Nederend, M., Penninx, L., Tajik, M., and Boom, J. (2014). The teacher's role in supporting young children's level of play engagement. *Early Child Development and Care, 184*(8): 1233–49.

Snyder, C., (2017). Embracing the power of play: The active learners. *HighScope Journal of Early Educators.* Retrieved from https://highscopre.org/the-active-learner.

Special Education Guide. (2017a). *Early identification: How the child find program works.* Retrieved from https://www.specialeducationguide.com/early-intervention/early-identification-how-the-child-find-program-works/.

———. (2017b). *The steps in early intervention.* Retrieved from https://www.specialeducationguide.com/early-intervention/steps-in-early-intervention-idea-part-c/.

———. (2017c). *The who, what, why of an individual family service plan.* Retrieved from https://www.specialeducationguide.com/early-intervention/the-who-what-why-of-an-individual-family-services-plan-ifsp/.

Special Education News. (2017). *IDEIA-individuals with disabilities education improvement act.* Retrieved from http://www.specialednews.com/special-education-dictionary/ideia-individuals-with-disabilities-education-improvement-act.htm.

Speech-Language & Audiology Canada. (2017). *What do speech-language pathologists do?* Retrieved from http://www.sac-oac.ca/public/what-do-speech-language-pathologists-do.

Spivey, B.L. (2017). *What are developmental domains?* Retrieved from http://www.handyhandouts.com/viewHandout.aspx?hh_number=358&nfp_title=What.

Stancill, J. (2016). *Study: NC preschool programs yield long-lasting gains for children.* Retrieved from http://www.charlotteobserver.com/news/local/education/article115728038.html.

Stanton-Chapman, T. L., and Brown, T. (2015). A strategy to increase the social interactions of 3-year-old children with disabilities in an inclusive classroom. *Topics in Early Childhood Special Education, 35*(1): 4–14.

Stuss, D. T. (2011). Functions of the frontal lobes: Relation to executive functions. *Journal of the International Neuropsychological Society, 17*, 759–65.

Success Music Studio. (n.d.). *What are multisensory techniques?* Retrieved from http://www.successmusicstudio.com/?page_id=80.

Suitts, S., Barba, P., and Dunn, K. (2015). *Research bulletin: A new majority; low income students now a minority in the nation's public schools.* Southern Education Foundation. Retrieved from www.southerneducation.org.

Tarrant. (2017). *Intellectual & developmental disabilities: Augmentative and alternative communication.* Retrieved from http://tarrant.tx.networkofcare.org/dd/assistive/list.aspx?indexingterms=augmentative-and-alternative-communication.

Tobin, J., Arzubiaga, A. E., and Adair, J. F. (2013). *Children crossing borders: Immigrant parent and teacher perspectives on preschool.* New York: Russell Sage Foundation.

Tran, Y. (2014). Addressing reciprocity between families and schools: Why these bridges are instrumental for students' academic success. *Faculty Publications-School of Education*. Retrieved from http://digitialcommons.georgefox.edu/soe_faculty/99.

Troseth, G. L., Russo, C. E., and Strouse, G. A. (2016). What's next for research on young children's interactive media? *Journal of Children and Media, 10*(1): 54–62. doi: 10.1080/17482798.2015.1123166.

Turner-Vorbeck, T. A. (2013). *Expanding multicultural education to include family diversity*. Retrieved from ProQuest Central database.

UNICEF. (2013). *Children and young people with disabilities fact sheet*. Retrieved from https://www.unicef.org/disabilities/files/Factsheet_A5__Web_NEW.pdf.

United Cerebral Palsy. (2017a). *Home modification*. Retrieved from http://www.mychildwithoutlimits.org/plan/assistive-technology/home-modification/.

———. (2017b). *The difference between an IFSP and an IEP*. Retrieved from http://www.mychildwithoutlimits.org/plan/early-intervention/ifsp-iep-comparison/.

U.S. Department of Agriculture (USDA), Food and Nutrition Service. (2017a). *Child and Adult Care Food Program*. Retrieved from https://www.fns.usda.gov/cacfp/meals-and-snacks.

———. (2017b). *The National School Lunch Program*. Retrieved from https://www.fns.usda.gov/cacfp/meals-and-snacks.

U.S. Department of Education. (n.d.a). *IDEA 2004: Building the legacy: Part C (birth—2 years old)*. Retrieved from http://idea.ed.gov/part-c/search/new.html.

———. (n.d.b). *Protecting students with disabilities*. Retrieved from https://www2.ed.gov/about/offices/list/ocr/504faq.html.

———. (2007). *Family education rights privacy act*. Retrieved from https://www2.ed.gov/policy/gen/guid/fpco/brochures/parents.html.

———. (2012). *Serving preschool children through title I: part A of the Elementary and Secondary Education Act of 1965, as amended*. Retrieved from https://www2.ed.gov/policy/elsec/guid/preschoolguidance2012.pdf.

———. (2014). *Questions and answers regarding inclusion of English learners with disabilities in English language proficiency assessments*. Retrieved from https://www2.ed.gov/about/offices/list/osers/news-2014.html.

———. (2015). *A matter of equity: Preschool in America*. Retrieved from https://www2.ed.gov/documents/early-learning/matter-equity-preschool-america.pdf.

U.S. Department of Education and U.S. Department of Health and Human Services. (2017). *Policy statement on inclusion of young children with disabilities in early childhood programs*. Retrieved from https://www2.ed.gov/policy/speced/guid/earlylearning/joint-statement-executivesummary.pdf.

———. (2017). *About the office of Head Start*. Retrieved from https://www.acf.hhs.gov/ohs/about.

U.S. Department of Health and Human Services and U.S. Department of Education. (2015). *Policy statement on inclusion of children with disabilities in early childhood programs*. Retrieved from https://www2.ed.gov/policy/speced/guid/earlylearning/joint-statement-full-text.pdf.

U.S. Department of Justice. (2017). *Commonly asked questions about child care centers and the Americans with Disabilities Act.* Retrieved from https://www.ada .gov/childqanda.htm.

U.S. Department of Justice, Civil Rights Division. (1990). *Information on technical assistance on the Americans with Disabilities act.* Retrieved from https://www.ada .gov/ada_intro.htm.

Vanderbilt University. (2017). *Teaching your child to: Identify and express emotions.* Retrieved from http://csefel.vanderbilt.edu/documents/teaching_emotions.pdf.

van Voorhis, F., Maier, M., Epstein, J., and Lloyd, C. (2013). *The impact of family involvement on the education of children ages 3–8: A focus on literacy and math achievement outcomes and social-emotional skills.* Retrieved from http://www .mdrc.org/publication/impact-family-involvement-education-children-ages-3-8.

Verdine, B. N., Irwin, C. M., Golinkoff, R, M., and Hirsh-Pasek, K. (2014). Contributions of executive function and spatial skills to preschool mathematics achievement. *Journal of Exceptional Children, 126,* 37–51. doi: 10.1016/j. jeep.2014.02.012.

Vergean, B. (2011). How extended families can support children with disabilities. *Birth Through 5 News.* Retrieved from http://www.birth23.org/files/b5news/ B52011Spring.pdf.

Vértes, P. E., and Bullmore, E. T. (2015). Annual research review: Growth connectomics—the organization and reorganization of brain networks during normal and abnormal development. *Journal of Child Psychology and Psychiatry, 56,* 299–320. doi:10.1111/jcpp.12365.

Vickers, B. (n.d.) *Behavioral issues and the use of social stories.* Bloomington: Indiana University.

Watson, S. (2017). *Tips for working with students in wheelchairs.* Retrieved from https://www.thoughtco.com/working-with-students-in-wheelchairs-3111137.

Wayland Free Public Library. (2017). *Our programs.* Retrieved from https:// waylandlibrary.org/our-programs/.

WebMD. (2017). *IEP for kids with disabilities.* Retrieved from https://www.webmd .com/add-adhd/childhood-adhd/adhd-iep-for-adhd#1.

Weiland, C., and Yoshikawa, H. (2013). Impacts of a prekindergarten program on children's mathematics, language, literacy, executive function, and emotional skills. *Child Development, 84*(6): 2112–30.

WIDA. (2014). *Focus on the early years: Dual language learners.* University of Wisconsin, Madison. Retrieved from https://www.wida.us/get.aspx?id=761.

Wight, V., Chau, M., and Aratani, Y. (2010). Who are America's poor children? The official story. National Center for Children in Poverty, 1–8. Columbia University.

Wood, E. A. (2013). Free choice and free play in early childhood education: Troubling the discourse. *International Journal of Early Years Education, 22*(1): 4–18. doi: 10.1080/09669760.2013.830562.

Wood, E. A., and Hall, E. (2011). Drawings as spaces for intellectual play. *International Journal of the Early Years Education, 19*(3–4): 267–81. Retrieved from http:// web.b.ebscohost.com.ezproxy.neu.edu/ehost/pdfviewer/pdfviewer?vid=10&sid= 8249a06a-11b4-43e3-80ab-ef1998d23813%40sessionmgr104.

Woodrow, C. (2014). Refocusing our attention to children's learning and the complex interplay of context and culture. *International Journal of Early Years Education,* *22*(1): 1–2. doi: 10.1080/09669760.2014.902639.

World Health Organization (WHO). (2011). *Summary: World report on disability.* Retrieved from http://apps.who.int/iris/bitstream/10665/70670/1/WHO_NMH_ VIP_11.01_eng.pdf.

————. (2012). *Early childhood development and disability: A discussion paper.* Retrieved from http://apps.who.int/iris/bitstream/10665/75355/1/9789241504065_ eng.pdf.

Wright, P. W. D., and Wright, P. D. (2016). *Child find.* Retrieved from http://www .wrightslaw.com/info/child.find.index.htm.

Yoshikawa, H., Weiland, C., Brooks-Gunn, J., Burchinal, M. R., Espinosa, L. M., Gormley, W. T., and Zaslow, M. J. (2013). *Investing in our future: The evidence base on preschool education.* Society for Research in Child Development. New York: Foundation for Child Development. Retrieved from https://www.fcd-us.org/ the-evidence-base-on-preschool/.

Young, N. D., Bonanno-Sotiropoulus, K., and Smolinski, J. A. (2018). *Making the grade: Promoting positive outcomes for student with learning disabilities.* Lanham, MD: Rowman & Littlefield.

Young, N. D., and Celli, L. M. (2014). *Learning style perspectives: Impact in the classroom* (3rd ed.). Madison, WI: Atwood Publishing.

Zand, D., Pierce, K., Thomson, N., Baig, M. W., Teodorescu, C., Nibras, S., and Maxim, R. (2014). Social competence in infants and toddlers with special health care needs: The roles of parental knowledge, expectations, attunement, and attitudes toward child independence. *Children, 1*(1): 5–20. Retrieved from http:// www.mdpi.com/2227-9067/1/1/5.

About the Authors

Dr. Nicholas D. Young has worked in diverse educational roles for more than thirty years, serving as a principal, special education director, graduate professor, graduate program director, graduate dean, and longtime superintendent of schools. He was named the Massachusetts Superintendent of the Year, and he completed a distinguished Fulbright program focused on the Japanese educational system through the collegiate level. Dr. Young is the recipient of numerous other honors and recognitions, including the General Douglas MacArthur Award for distinguished civilian and military leadership and the Vice Admiral John T. Hayward Award for exemplary scholarship. He holds several graduate degrees, including a PhD in educational administration and an EdD in educational psychology.

Dr. Young has served in the US Army and US Army Reserves, combined, for over thirty-four years, and he graduated with distinction from the US Air War College, the US Army War College, and the US Navy War College. After completing a series of senior leadership assignments in the US Army Reserves as the commanding officer of the 287th Medical Company (DS), the 405th Area Support Company (DS), the 405th Combat Support Hospital, and the 399th Combat Support Hospital, he transitioned to his current military position as a faculty instructor at the US Army War College in Carlisle, Pennsylvania. He currently holds the rank of colonel.

Dr. Young is also a regular presenter at state, national, and international conferences, and he has written many books, book chapters, and articles on various topics in education, counseling, and psychology. Some of his most recent books include *Sounding the Alarm in the Schoolhouse: Safety, Security and Student Well-Being* (in-press); *Embracing and Educating the Autistic Child: Valuing Those Who Color Outside the Lines* (in-press); *Potency of the Principalship: Action-Oriented Leadership for School Improvement* (in-press); *The Soul of the Schoolhouse: Cultivating Student Engagement* (in-press); *Captivating Classrooms: Student Engagement at the Heart of School Improvement* (in-press); *Guardian of the Next Generation: Igniting the Passion for Quality Teaching* (2018); *From Head to Heart: High Quality Teaching Practices in the Spotlight* (2018); *Stars in the Schoolhouse: Teaching Practices and Approaches that Make a Difference* (2018); *Achieving Results: Maximizing Student Success in the Schoolhouse* (2018); *Dog Tags to Diploma: Understanding and Addressing the Educational Needs of Veterans, Service Members, and their Families* (in press); *Making the Grade: Promoting Positive Outcomes for Students with Learning Disabilities* (2018); *Paving the Pathway for Educational Success: Effective Classroom Interventions for Students with Learning Disabilities* (2018); *Wrestling with Writing: Effective Strategies for Struggling Students* (2018); *Floundering to Fluent: Reaching and Teaching the Struggling Student* (2018); *From Lecture Hall to Laptop: Opportunities, Challenges, and the Continuing Evolution of Virtual Learning in Higher Education* (2017); *Emotions and Education: Promoting Positive Mental Health in Students with Learning* (2017); *The Power of the Professoriate: Demands, Challenges, and Opportunities in 21st Century Higher Education* (2017); *To Campus with Confidence: Supporting a Successful Transition to College for Students with Learning Disabilities* (2017); *Educational Entrepreneurship: Promoting Public-Private Partnerships for the 21st Century* (2015); *Beyond the Bedtime Story: Promoting Reading Development during the Middle School Years* (2015); *Betwixt and Between: Understanding and Meeting the Social and Emotional Developmental Needs of Students During the Middle School Transition Years* (2014); *Learning Style Perspectives: Impact upon the Classroom* (3rd ed., 2014); *Collapsing Educational Boundaries from Preschool to PhD: Building Bridges across the Educational Spectrum* (2013); *Transforming Special Education Practices: A Primer for School Administrators and Policy Makers* (2012); and *Powerful Partners in Student Success: Schools, Families and Communities* (2012). He also coauthored several children's books, to include the popular series *I Am Full of Possibilities.* Dr. Young may be contacted directly at nyoung1191@aol.com.

Dr. Elizabeth Jean has served as an elementary school educator and administrator in various rural and urban settings in Massachusetts for more than twenty years. As a building administrator, she has been instrumental in fostering partnerships with various local businesses and higher education institutions. Further, she is currently a graduate adjunct professor at Endicott College and previously taught at Our Lady of the Elms College. Dr. Jean received a BS in education from Springfield College; an MEd in education with a concentration in reading from Our Lady of the Elms; and an EdD in curriculum, teaching, learning, and leadership from Northeastern University.

Dr. Jean's books include *Stars in the Schoolhouse: Teaching Practices and Approaches that Make a Difference* (2018); *From Head to Heart: High Quality Teaching Practices in the Spotlight* (2018); *Dog Tags to Diploma: Understanding and Addressing the Educational Needs of Veterans, Service Members, and their Families* (in press) and *From Lecture Hall to Laptop: Opportunities, Challenges and the Continuing Evolution of Virtual Learning in Higher Education* (2017). She has also written book chapters on such topics as emotional well-being for students with learning disabilities, parental supports for students with learning disabilities, public and private partnerships in public education, technology partnerships between K–12 and higher education, home school partnerships, cultural connections, developing a strategic mindset for LD students, the importance of skill and will in developing reading habits for young children, and middle school reading interventions, to name a few. Additionally, she has coauthored and illustrated several children's books, to include *Yes, Mama* (2018), *The Adventures of Scotty the Skunk: What's that Smell?* (2014), and the *I am Full of Possibilities* series. She may be contacted at elizabethjean1221@gmail.com.

Dr. Anne E. Mead has more than thirty-five years of experience in the early childhood education field. Her career has spanned professional roles as a family childcare provider, childcare center director, preschool special education instructor, early childhood education trainer, and consultant on organizational and system management. Dr. Mead is currently the administrator for early childhood programs and extended learning for the Danbury Public Schools in Danbury, Connecticut. In this district, she has been credited with the development of a family and community engagement center, before- and after-school programs, and the formation of a family learning center. Dr. Mead is a biweekly contributor to the *Tribuna* newspaper, where she has specialized in writing regional articles on family engagement and child education and development. She received a BA in human services from the University of Connecticut, an MEd in educational leadership from National Louis University, and an EdD in organizational leadership studies from Northeastern University. Dr. Mead has served on numerous local and state boards related to early childhood education and was a founding member of the National Association for Family, School and Community Engagement. She is a member of the Campaign for Grade Level Reading and serves on the family engagement design team for the State of Connecticut State Department of Education. Dr. Mead may be contacted at annemead2003@yahoo.com.